Family Reunion

TAKING IT INTO THE NEXT LEVEL

REGINA MASON

Copyright @2022 by Regina Mason

All rights reserved. No part of this book may be reproduced in any form or by any electronic or mechanical means, including information storage and retrieval systems, without permission in writing from the publisher, except by reviewers, who may quote brief passages in a review.

This publication contains the opinions and ideas of its author. It is intended to provide helpful and informative material on the subjects addressed in the publication. The author and publisher specifically disclaim all responsibility for any liability, loss or risk, personal or otherwise, which is incurred as a consequence, directly or indirectly, of the use and application of any of the contents of this book.

WORKBOOK PRESS LLC
187 E Warm Springs Rd,
Suite B285, Las Vegas, NV 89119, USA

Website:	https://workbookpress.com/
Hotline:	1-888-818-4856
Email:	admin@workbookpress.com

Ordering Information:
Quantity sales. Special discounts are available on quantity purchases by corporations, associations, and others.
For details, contact the publisher at the address above.

Library of Congress Control Number:

ISBN-13:   000-0-000000-00-0 (Paperback Version)
            000-0-000000-00-0 (Digital Version)

REV. DATE: 06/05/2022

Dedication

First and foremost, I would like to dedicate this book to my Lord and Savior, Jesus Christ. For without Him, this book would not have been possible. My faith in Jesus has given me the inspiration, wisdom, guidance, and direction in writing this book. Bishop David G. Evans, Senior Pastor of Bethany Baptist Church has in more ways than one been a source of encouragement and motivation in starting this project. In the short time that I have been a member of Bethany, Bishop Evans has been a spiritual mentor and coach. In his powerful and poignant messages, he has help to awaken the God-given gifts in me that were once dormant. Bishop Evans, thank you for all that you do and how you motivate us to excellence. I would also like to dedicate this book to all the descendants of the Reeder Family. Back in 1990 when I first began my journey in researching the family history, I never imagined that eighteen years later, our family reunions would still be going strong. During the summer of 2010, at our eleventh national reunion, we had 108 attendees from five different branches. Relatives came from near and far. They came from as far west as California and as far east as New York. We had representatives from ten states and the District of Columbia. Over the years, our family has been committed in supporting our reunions. Reeder family, this one's for you. Thanks for being one of the inspirations for this book. It would be remiss of me not to mention my late aunt Earnestine Dawson, who was a trailblazer with regards to keeping our family's history alive. In fact, she was the first family member that participated in the formal oral history interview. It was from the information that she shared that I was able to embark on my journey of genealogical discovery. She was the one that told me about my maternal descendants dating back to my great-great-grandmother.

This history was the single most important piece of the puzzle that connected our family's roots back to its origins in Ethiopia, Africa. Not only was my aunt probably one of our family's historians, she was the one who traveled year after year across the United States, visiting family members from near and far. Whenever traveling to a state where there was family, Aunt Earnestine would set time out of her schedule to visit and spend time with our relatives. When she came to visit our family every summer, Aunt Earnestine would often share stories about her visits with our relatives. Looking back, I appreciate all that she did to preserve our history and to instill a sense of family connectedness in me. I write this book Haley (August 11, 1921-February 10, 1992), the very famous African American writer best known as the author of Roots: The Saga of an American Family. Alex Haley was most inspirational for me in my quest for learning about my family roots and the writing of this book. In 1976, Haley published Roots: The Saga of an American Family, a novel based on his family's history, starting with the story of Kunta Kinte, kidnapped in The Gambia in 1767 and transported to the Province of Maryland to be sold as a slave. Haley had reported to be a seventh-generation descendant of Kunta Kinte, and his work on the novel involved ten years of research, intercontinental travel, and *writing (Source: http://en.wikipedia.org/wiki/Alex_Haley)*. I, too, was fortunate to have been able to travel to West Africa in 1991. On this trip, I had visited Senegal, The Gambia, and Gorée Island. This trip changed my life forever. Not only was it a trip of self-discovery, I learned of the tribe my family came from that was, years later, confirmed by DNA testing. Although Alex Haley is no longer with us, he was a great pioneer the field of genealogy research and connecting families to their roots. He sparked an interest in genealogy research not only within me, but millions of other Americans as well. Alex Haley, this book is dedicated to you as well.

Acknowledgments

Planning a family reunion is a major undertaking. It requires committed and dedicated people to ensure its success. The success of the Reeder family reunion would not be possible without strong leaders. There are two individuals I would like to especially thank. First would be my brother, Elijah Mason. In the seventeen years that we have held our reunions, he has worked tirelessly as the national president of our reunion planning committee. His duties range from making sure the regional presidents stay on track with reunion plans to coordinating local family activities even between national reunions. In addition to all these responsibilities, he is our family photographer. Elijah, thanks for all you do to keep the family bonded together. Second, I would like to acknowledge my cousin Deborah Scott. She has been largely responsible for maintaining and updating the computer database of our descendants. Additionally, Deborah has prepared our family's tree for display at our reunions. She too has been a source of support for various regional planning committee members. Deborah, I personally thank you for your time and dedication over the years to assure the success of our family's reunions. Finally, to all my family who were actively involved on the reunion planning committees, I would like to say thank you to you as well. Without all of your support, our reunions would not be possible.

Introduction

As I was updating my family's history in preparation for our most recent reunion, it was hard for me to believe that seventeen years ago we had our first national reunion and we are still going strong. Currently, we have been able to identify over one thousand relatives in our family tree with eight generations represented. Over the years, I have often encountered individuals who were impressed with our family reunions and wanted me to share advice with them on planning their own reunion. These individuals would often ask me about the steps involved in planning a reunion for over fifty relatives and from multiple branches of the family tree. Consequently, the idea came to me to write this book. I thought, if I put all that I learned through trial and error over the past twenty years into a book, many people would benefit from my experiences. Also, the time spent in researching the various genealogy and family reunion resources on the market would be practically eliminated through my book. So, now let's delve into this exciting journey of how I got involved in genealogy research and family reunion planning. Initially, the research of my family's health history began as a project to learn more about what conditions and diseases were prevalent in our family. My background as a nurse practitioner was the impetus for obtaining this information. Those of us who are health care providers are aware of the value of knowing one's family health history. Family history can help to predict an individual's risk of developing diseases like cancer. Genetics does play a role in what diseases a person might succumb to. By knowing what diseases and conditions were present in my family, I thought that I would be better able to communicate health risks with the purpose of disease prevention. Little did I know, twenty years later, that this project would turn into something greater than I ever could have anticipated. Not only am I the family historian, I also function as the genealogical researcher and provide informal consultations in family reunion planning. This book is a step-by-step guide book designed to help both the novice and seasoned family historian and reunion organizer navigate through the process of successful genealogy research and family reunion planning. Successful family reunion planning must always begin with the family history. The family history is the glue that binds the family together. Once family members understand how they are related to one another, a sense of connectedness and unity will soon follow. This book reviews the methods for researching your family's history. After any individual can take their family reunion to the next level. Taking your family reunion to the next level involves going from the backyard to hotel courtyard, local to national level, and one branch to include multiple branches of the family tree. This book will answer some very important questions that will help you to plan a successful reunion. How do I begin the process of researching my family's history? What and how many committees are needed to plan a reunion? How do you keep the interest alive year after year? These questions, and many more, will be answered to help you plan a memorable and fun family reunion. The focus of this book will be on planning a larger scale family reunion for fifty or more attendees.

Chapter 1

Defining Family History and Its Importance History is simply the study of the past events. Wikipedia defines family history as the systematic narrative and research of past events relating to a specific family. It is a broad term with many facets that incorporates genealogy, genetics, surname and place (of origin) studies, clan research, and oral histories, just to name a few. The one area of family history research that we probably are most familiar with is genealogy. As we know, genealogy is the study of one's ancestors. This involves tracing a living or historic person's ancestry back into time from the present using archival records.

(Source:http://www.merriam-webster.com/dictionary/history, http://en.wikipedia.org/wiki/Family_history).

Marcus Garvey, an African Nationalist and publicist coined the phrase "A people without the knowledge of their past history, origin, and culture is like a tree without roots." This saying is understood by historians and genealogists alike. Let us consider the analogy of tree. When we examine the purpose of a tree's roots, we find that it is to firmly anchor it in the ground, allowing it to grow (Source: http://wiki.answers.com/Q/ What is the purpose of the roots). Similarly, one's family history is like the roots of a tree. When we learn of our family's history, it grounds us and shapes our lives as individuals. Drawing from the past experiences of our ancestors helps us to learn from their successes and failures. In this process of learning about our past history, we can improve upon our future. For example, in my family, a college education is highly valued. Many of our second and third-generation descendants were farm laborers in South Carolina and not able to acquire a college education. Because I heard the stories of how hard they worked to maintain their farms, I chose a professional career. My relatives would often tell me, "Go as far as you can go" when referring to my educational endeavors and aspirations. I strongly believe that the knowledge I acquired about my family's history at a young age played a major role in shaping my life today. Family history also provides us with a greater sense of self-identity. When we know where we have come from, we will have a fuller understanding of who we are. Some twenty years ago when I began to seriously embark on the study of my family's history, I must admit that I was experiencing a bit of an identity crisis. I wanted to answer that age-old questions, "Who am I? and where did I come from?" In my opinion, Alex Haley described this desire better than anyone that I loneliness." He understood the importance of family history and its connection to our self-identity. His book Roots and later the popular television mini-series changed America. He told the story of millions of African American families in his quest of self-identity through the lives of his ancestors. He traced his roots back to a village in West Africa. On his journey, Alex Haley discovers that he is a descendant of Kunta Kinte, a slave from the Mandinka tribe of The Gambia, who was eventually freed. I am sure that prior to the discovery of his family's rich heritage and history, he could not have even imagined the enduring strength of his ancestors. No doubt, learning about the history of his African descendants and all that they had to endure helped him to tap into this strength in his own life (Source:http://en.wikipedia.org/wiki/Roots:_The_Saga_of_an_American_Family , http://kintehaley.org/foundationhistory.html). My story parallels that of Alex Haley's.

Encouraged and motivated by his story, I too journeyed to West Africa in 1991. When I arrived, my purpose was to find whatever information I could about my African ancestry. I had often listened to stories that my aunt Earnestine would tell about my maternal great-great-grandmother who was from Ethiopia, Africa. Not much was known about her except that she had a son fathered by a white slave master and later settled in Newberry, South Carolina from Africa. She later married a man who was a Cherokee Indian and had twelve more children. She and my great-great-grandfather raised their children on a farmhouse in Newberry. More than likely, farming was the primary source of their livelihood. Both spent their last days in South Carolina. This information was just not enough for me. I wanted to know what tribe she was from in Africa. So, on a wing and prayer, I packed my bags and ended up in Senegal, The Gambia, and Gorée Island, West Africa. Traveling to Africa was an emotional experience for me. Quite frankly, when I arrived in West Africa, I had no idea where to even begin my research, so I began to question the natives about some of the tribal groups in Africa and how I could find out what tribe my ancestors were from. To my surprise, everyone that I interviewed told me the same thing; I was from the Fulani Tribe based on my facial features and bodily characteristics. Mind you, this was some years prior to DNA genealogy. I shared this information with my family when I returned, but did not fully trust the accuracy of the information that I had received. When I began to learn of DNA genealogy, I thought what a perfect way to finally confirm our family's maternal African ancestry. You will learn more about this technology in later chapters. At our family's reunion in 2010, we discussed our plan to purchase and conduct the DNA test. Our family graciously contributed to the funding of the test, which was $349. I was flabbergasted to learn that the information I was given in Africa was indeed correct and that my maternal ancestry was linked to Hausa-Fulani tribe in Nigeria, Africa. Learning more about these tribes, I discovered that the people of the Hausa-Fulani tribe were primarily cattle herders, who were nomads traveling from town to town to ensure that their cattle had grass to feed upon. I guess you may ask, how did this trip to Africa and learning about my roots provide me with a greater sense of self-identity? Let me share my thoughts with you. When I left Africa, I came away transformed, but found it difficult to put it into words. There is just something very special about the process of self-discovery through genealogy research. Yes, it anchored me in that I now felt firmly secured in who I was through learning about my African ancestry. Not just only knowing, but also being able to visit one of the original slave houses on Gorée Island, I was better able to envision the struggles that my great-great-grandmother endured being forced from a familiar land to an unfamiliar place, America, and surviving this experience. I was horrified to learn that millions of native Africans died en route to America, some due to cruel treatment and others from illness. So, then what I took away from this trip was that there was something innately in my great-great-grandmother that was passed down to me, the ability to overcome horrific circumstances and come out a winner. In sum, during my trip to Africa, I learned I had great survivor skills that surpass human understanding. And yes, if my great-great-grandmother made it, then I can too. Additionally, I discovered I was from the Hausa-Fulani Tribe, which led to future research and studies about this tribe and their origin. What a rich heritage I received. As previously mentioned, when I returned from Africa, I did share what I learned with other relatives with the full understanding that another great benefit of family history is the ability to create a legacy for future generations. Just imagine, if Aunt Earnestine had not passed down what she knew about our family's history to me and others, the link between these generations would have been lost and those precious memories long forgotten. How tragic this would be for the present and the future generations not to know that such rich and strong legacy of survivorship existed. Thus far, we have learned that family history helps to ground us, shaping our future; provides us with a greater sense of self-identity, and creates a legacy for future generations to draw from. Family history is also important in playing a role disease himself. And if both his father and his grandfather had it, the risk jumps to nine times. Put it another way, if your father or grandfather had prostate cancer before age of fifty-five, your risk of getting it is 50 percent (Source: "Evidence for a Prostate Cancer Susceptibility Locus on the X Chromosome." Xu, J; Heyers, D; Freije, D; Isaacs, S; et al. Nature Genetics, Vol. 20: 175-179, 1998 and http://www.malehealthcenter.com/m_topics.html). You ask what's good about knowing your risk for getting prostate cancer? It's simple. It is far better than not knowing. Prostate cancer, like other types of cancers can grow fairly slowly, and it can be cured entirely if detected early. A key to early detection is screening for prostate cancer at the appropriate age. For example, a man at average risk for prostate cancer should be screened at age fifty. Average risk means no family history of prostate cancer. However, men at higher risk, including African American men and those with a first-degree relative (father or brother) diagnosed with prostate cancer before age sixty-five, should be screened for prostate cancer beginning at age forty-five. Men at appreciably higher risk (multiple family members diagnosed with prostate cancer before age sixty-five) should begin to be screened for prostate cancer beginning at age forty. Screening includes an annual digital rectal exam (gloved finger feeling the prostate gland for abnormalities) and a blood test called the PSA (Prostate-specific antigen) which is a protein produced by cells of the prostate gland. The PSA test measures the level of PSA in the blood and it may be higher than normal in men who have prostate cancer. Thus, it pays to know your genetic road map and take a few simple steps to avoid road hazards (Source: http://www.cancer.org/AboutUs/DrLensBlog/post/2010/03/03/New-Prostate-Cancer-Screening-Guidelines.aspx, http://www.malehealthcenter.com/m_topics.html, http://www.cancer.gov/cancertopics/factsheet/detection/PSA). Now, for one final reason why family history is important is that it is a vital part of reunion planning. Actually, the success of your reunion is based on how much is known about the family's history and passed on to future generations. Once family members understand how they are related to one another, a sense of connectedness and unity will develop. I can recall when we were planning our first national reunion back in 1992-1993, our planning committee believed that it was especially important to display a poster-sized version of family with all 13 branches listed. This was important since many of the 103 reunion attendees would be meeting for the first time. I certainly believed this played a major factor in the continued success of our family reunions. Creative ways to preserve and share your family's history will be addressed later in this book.

Chapter 2

Family History Research—Preparation Phase

One question that I am asked most often by people I encounter who have an interest in tracing their family roots and or planning a family reunion is "Where do I start?" In the introduction it was mentioned that before you can even begin to think about planning a reunion, you must know and be able to share your family's history so that once your family comes together at the reunion, they will understand how they are related to one another. It is this knowledge of connectedness that fosters a sense of unity. In the next few sections, we will explore the steps involved in the process of researching your family's history. Phase one is the preparation phase that involves searching for in-home family history records and documents such as birth and death certificates, obituaries, wedding announcement, or scrapbooks. Once you have gathered the various documents and records in your possession, the next phase of family history research is the most important, that is, getting organized. Completing pedigree charts and family group sheets/records is a good starting point for getting organized. Utilization of genealogy software, however, is the quickest and most efficient way available today to organize all of your family's history after you have completed the pedigree charts and family group sheets/records. Even after you have filled out your pedigree charts and family groups sheets/records as far as your current information will allow, you will find that there are many blanks left on your sheets. There will be many things you never knew about your relatives that will lead you to research other sources of data including, but not limited to, oral histories, genealogy records and databases, and DNA tests. We will now draw our attention to the three phases of family history research—preparation, organization, and data collection. Researching the family history can be a daunting and time-consuming task. Anyone who decides to embark on this journey should be in it for the long haul. Ideally, you only need two committed people who share mutual interest in genealogical research to function in role of family historians. The responsibility of the family historian includes, being in charge of coordinating and presenting family history information. However, you should solicit the help of other relatives whenever possible. Later in this book, I will address the role of the history and research committee. Must start with yourself, and then work in back to earlier generations. I recommend that you start with writing a biography of yourself. Carefully record the important facts of your own life and what you know of your parents and grandparents. You should continue your research as far back as you can go.

Surveying Family Records and Documents

The next step in researching your family's history is gaining access to the family documents and records. There are two basic categories of genealogy records to search; compiled and original. Compiled consist of those genealogy records of previous research, created by others including family histories and biographies. Original are those created at or near the time of an event, such birth, marriage, death, or census records. The primary records that you should begin to gather first are birth certificates, marriage licenses, and death certificates followed by obituaries, baptismal records, personal family letters, newspaper clippings, social security cards, military records, deeds, wills, and estate and medical records. An often forgotten source of documents, records, and photos are family bibles. Many families once used the family's bible to document important events such as births of children, baptismal information, and to store family photographs. Old letters are important sources of information. Pay special attention to the addresses on envelopes, and the dates the letters were posted. A letter that my mother had saved twenty years prior to planning our reunion was the key in locating distant relatives from various branches of our family's tree. So, never underestimate the value of any document that you collect.

Chapter 3

Family History Research — Organizational Phase

(Source: http://www.experiencefestival.com/wp/article/research-your-history-and-create-a-family-tree, http://www.ehow.com/about_5297174_pedigree-chart-used.html#ixzz1FnAYWbYF) After you have collected all of your family's resources, you need the appropriate tools to help you to organize this data in a formal, concise, and easy to use manner. There will be three main tools used by genealogists that you will find beneficial, that is, pedigree charts, family group sheets/records, and genealogy software.

Pedigree Charts

The pedigree chart is one of the basic tools used for recording your genealogy. It shows the direct bloodlines of ancestors that it begins with you and extends to your parents, grandparents, great-grandparents, and so forth. It also is a graphical representation of how the family fits and is related to each other and usually includes four generations on a page. Refer to the Web site http://genealogy.about.com/library/free_charts/pedigree.pdf for a free downloadable pedigree chart. Your family's information can be typed in right from your computer browser, making this free genealogy pedigree chart very handy for sharing your family tree with friends and relatives. Once the information has been typed in, the form can be saved locally to your computer, e-mailed to family and friends, or printed out. Pedigree charts have the benefit of allowing you to see several generations of family members at a glance on one sheet. Pedigree charts are the basic units, but you will want to produce family group sheets for all of your entries http://www.helium.com/items/1152386-how-to-use-a-pedigree-chart).

How to Complete a Pedigree Chart?

First list your name, the creator of the chart, in the position #1 on the chart. Next, fill in your birth date, place of birth, spouse's name, and marriage date. This step should be repeated for father and mother, position #2 and # 3, respectively not forgetting to include dates of death. Be sure to always use maiden names for any female listed on your chart. After entering your parents, then you enter the information of the parents of your parents' parents and keep going. After you finish the first page, you will have yourself, parents, grandparents, great-grandparents (Source: *http//genealogy.about.com/od/free_charts/a/forms.htm*).

Family Group Sheet/Record

The Family Group Sheet is used to include vital information for one family group and allow room to include information on the children of your ancestors, along with their spouses. These collateral lines can prove to be important when tracing your family tree, providing another source of information on your ancestors. For example, if you have difficulty locating a birth record for your own ancestors, you may be able to learn the names of his parents through the birth record of his brother. The family group sheet lists the father and mother at the top, with all of the children, from that union, listed on the bottom half of the sheet. Most family group sheets will ask for names of former spouses. Complete a new family group sheet for each marriage. At a minimum, complete four family group sheets, one with you as father or mother, another with you listed as one of the children, and the other two showing your parents as children. If you have adult children, complete family group sheets for each, showing their spouse's information and the children that they have together. The Web site http://c.mfcreative.com/pdf/trees/charts/ca/famgrec.pdf has a free downloadable family group record/sheet that allows you to input your family's information from your computer browser to be easily shared by others or saved on your computer. Pedigree charts and family group sheets work conjointly. For each marriage included on your pedigree chart, you will also complete a family group sheet. The pedigree chart provides an simple overview of your family tree, while the family group sheets provide further details on each generation (Source: http://genealogy.about.com/od/free_charts/a/forms.htm).

Genealogy Software—Putting It All Together

Now that you have completed your pedigree charts and family group sheets/records, you are ready to start in inputting your family's history information into the genealogy software. When I started my research over twenty years ago, genealogy software was virtually unheard-of and not readily available as it is today. Initially, I utilized the pen and paper method of documentation, but found it to be very time consuming and greatly limited what I could do with this information. I eventually did find a genealogy software package—Family Tree Maker—that was a wonderful discovery. Since our family had just begun to embark on planning our family reunion, Family Tree Maker had many features that I had found very useful. After inputting all of my relatives' names into the family tree, it was easy for me to build family group sheet/records, print out a calendar of birthdays, and best of all, I was able to design various versions of the family tree chart that was displayed at our family reunion. My cousin, Deborah Scott, who lived in Georgia, also had Family Tree Maker and was instrumental in designing a giant wall-sized family tree at the reunion. Our family loved the family tree poster because everyone could see how they were related to each other. As you can see, the main advantage of using genealogy software is what you can do with the information once it has been entered and saved. Genealogy software provides tools that make it easy to build your pedigree charts, family group records, record memories, organize family photos, and other important documents. Some software enables users to upload recorded oral histories, including videos and audio clips, in a way that facilitates the sharing of this information with other family members both online and offline. In the next few sections, the main features of various genealogy software packages will be reviewed and discussed in detail to help you learn which options best fit your family's needs.

What do you want the software to do?

The first order of business before selecting the appropriate software to build your family's tree is to decide what it is you want the software to achieve. Some software does the basics—building a family tree, storing data about your ancestors, and allowing you to print charts and reports—and they do them very well. While other software packages provide more adventurous features, which may be better suited for advanced users as opposed to beginners. After reading the next few sections, I believe you will be better able to make an informed decision about what genealogy software to choose.

Genealogy Software Features

Photos and Media

One of the most exciting aspects of researching your family history is discovering old photographs that let you know what your ancestors were really like, and how they lived. Whatever genealogy software that you choose, be sure to select one that will allow you to combine various types of media (photographs, audio, videos, and spreadsheets) to enhance the building of your family's tree. Look for software that lets you integrate photos within your research and then allow you to edit these photos within the program. By doing so, you can use all your research in a variety of publishable materials (Source: http://genealogy-websites.no1reviews.com/buying-guide.html).

Genealogy Research and Web Integration

You will find that quite a few genealogy software companies on the market today have Web sites devoted to genealogical research. One of the greatest advantages of perform searches of the best genealogical information, without having to leave the program itself (Source: http://genealogy-websites.no1reviews.com/buying-guide.html).

Research Tools

One of the most challenging areas of genealogy research is knowing exactly what to do with your information once it's been collected, this is especially true for the novice researcher. Some genealogy software packages offer features that you may never use but is helpful to know about possibly for the future. Research tools called a "Toolbox" offers functions that is supposed to help you make the most out of your research. Included in the toolbox can be the time line feature, which allows you to plot the major events in the lives of your ancestors. Also, you may find migration maps, which allow you to visually observe where you ancestors came from and where they went afterwards. Additionally, statistics generators allow you to view detailed statistics related to your family tree. I personally have not found any of these features helpful at the beginner level and have not found a need to use them (Source: http://genealogy-websites.no1reviews.com/buying-guide.html).

Advanced Features

Many software packages include a range of more advanced features, perfect for those who are more seasoned when it comes to family tree building and genealogical research. The GPS/Latitude-Longitude feature allows its users to pinpoint where ancestors used to live, and store this information within the family tree. It is likely that this technology will not be useful to many but was worthwhile to mention (Source: http://genealogy-websites.no1reviews.com/buying-guide.html).

Ease of Use and Navigation

I believe that one of the most important features of any genealogy software that you choose should be its ease of use and navigation. This is especially important for a novice computer user and one just embarking on genealogy research. The best way that I have found to check out how easy it is to use a particular software package is review the product and its features online. Some software companies offer online tutorials, Webinars, and free short-term trial offers which most people would find beneficial. Family Tree Maker has some of the best tutorials and Webinars (web-based seminars) that I have reviewed. Family Tree Maker 2011 is now available in Mac as well as IBM-PC compatible versions (Source: http://familytreemaker.com/Views/ Home/Home.aspx and http://genealogy-websites.no1reviews.com/buying-guide.html).

Updating

Some of the more popular genealogy software packages allow

users to update their programs (either for a nominal fee) when a product update is released. Software companies also allow users to purchase the new versions of their software (when a substantial product overhaul occurs) at a reduced rate. The capacity to update your software when new features are added is important and should be taken into consideration when choosing genealogy software (Source: http://genealogy-websites.no1reviews.com/buying-guide.html).

Books, Charts, Reports, Gifts, and More

As mentioned previously, one of the most exciting aspects of genealogy research that I have found is being able to share all of your family's history with other relatives in creative formats. Whether it is family photos, family books, charts, reports, and gifts (for example mugs and calendars) from a dedicated online store, these custom items are fun to create and can be a wonderful way to display the fruits of your research (Source: http://genealogy-websites.no1reviews.com/buying-guide.html).

Online/Offline Support and FAQs

Through some trial and error, I would venture to say that most genealogy software on the market today is fairly simple to use and it's unlikely to cause you many problems. However, it is recommended that you always choose genealogy software that comes complete with some form of support. I personally like online, as well as telephone support. Moreover, you should look for software that offers a listing of FAQs (frequently asked questions) to help you solve common issues (Source: http://genealogy-websites.no1reviews.com/buying-guide.html).

Genealogy Software Reviews

When reviewing the various genealogy software packages on the market, I became overwhelmed with the sheer numbers available to users today. Fortunately, I found a Web site called No1Reviews.com that took care of this daunting task. No1Reviews is owned and operated by Cyberscape Media and was established in the summer of 2006. This organization was founded for users looking for both expert editorial reviews and user reviews for software that includes genealogy. No1Reviews.com aims is to provide in-depth expert reviews alongside its user reviews for a broad range of products and services. This organization claims to http://genealogy-websites.no1reviews.com/buying-guide.html). So, let's examine their top three choices starting with their number one pick, Family Tree Maker 2011.

Family Tree Maker 2011

General Information

Family Tree Maker 2011 takes the number one Choice Award in the genealogy software category and is my personal favorite. It is offers a number of premium features and is part of the award-winning Ancestry.com group. No1Reviews.com has found Family Tree Maker 2011 to be ideally suited for both beginner and experienced genealogists. Family Tree Maker software also made Oprah's best pick for the holiday in December, 2010. At $39.95, it is very reasonably priced.

Ease of Use and Navigation

Family Tree Maker 2011 offers many possibilities when creating and managing your family tree. To begin with, it's extremely easy to create your own family tree, by entering your own personal information and then expanding the tree into the past by inputting all known information about your ancestors.

Genealogy Research and Web Integration

One of the best features of Family Tree Maker 2011 is that users can download their Ancestry.com family tree from their online account and merge it with an existing tree on Family Tree Maker 2011 and visa-versa. As Ancestry.com is the No. 1 rated genealogy Web site, certainly the combination of Ancestry.com and Family Tree Maker 2011 is a great opportunity for you to create a wonderful family tree.

Family Tree Maker 2011 also has improved performance with the importing of GEDCOM and .FTW files, and new features which allow you to view detailed statistics about the individuals in your tree, such as average life spans, earliest and latest birth dates, and more.

One of the features which really set Family Tree Maker 2011 apart from rival products is the Web dashboard. This has undergone numerous enhancements in the 2011 edition. First, the Web dashboard provides integration with Ancestry.com allowing automatic data sourcing from your account with Ancestry.com (or from the various free resources on Ancestry.com if you don't have an Ancestry.com subscription). This means that you don't need to use a Web browser to search for data separately and then manually enter it into the Family Tree Maker 2011 software, but can simply perform integrated searches within the software for specific information. You can also view twitter feeds from Ancestry.com and Family Tree Maker within your personal Web dashboard, to check out what is happening in the world of online genealogy.

Photos and Media

This software also supports a wide range of media additions to your family tree. One of the greatest pleasures in creating a family tree is looking at the various images that you collect through your research and sharing them with other members of your family. You will find numerous features that make adding media to your family tree extremely simple. There is also integrated scanner support, which allows you to add images directly to your family tree using your scanner.

You can also draw images directly from Ancestry.com and download them directly to your family tree. It's very simple to categorize and organize your media and create wonderful slideshows of your family history that are great to share with other members of your family. Finally, you can group media items to manage them as a group.

Advanced Features

Family Tree Maker 2011 also has a collection of advanced features intended to appeal to the more seasoned genealogist. You can take advantage of the GPS/Latitude-Longitude features to mark prominent locations in the lives of your ancestors on a digital map. The "Places Workspace" will allow you to access and modify GPS coordinates that are included in the statistics section of your family tree. You can add maps to your trees to illustrate the geographical distribution of your ancestry. Migration maps are also available so that you can plot the movement of your family throughout their lives. Finally, the offline "Places Authority" acts as a geographical encyclopedia or atlas, meaning you don't need to research the details of an ancestor's address—instead, simply look it up and automatically add the information to your family tree.

An additional advanced feature includes the Toolbox that contains a number of useful functions intended to make the process of creating your family tree easier. You can create time lines to plot the lives of your key ancestors, including their education, occupation, migration, marriage, and more, complete with images, maps, and data. The relationship calculator makes it easy to figure out how all of the members of your family tree are related to one another by simply clicking the relationship calculator. Furthermore, with the "Global Spell Checker" feature, you can rest assure that all names, place names, and workplaces are spelt correctly, even if they are written in foreign languages.

Books, Charts, Reports, and Gifts Additionally, you can create impressive books, reports, charts, and more using the dedicated Ancestry.com store. You can even use the images and diagrams featured in your family tree in a fun way to create beautiful gifts and materials for sharing with the rest of your family.

Family Tree Builder

General Information

Family Tree Builder 4.0 is the newest version of the Family Tree Builder software group produced by MyHeritage. This is a free "family networking" Web site with reportedly more than 33 million devoted users, and has received high rating reviews from No1Reviews.com. The nicest feature about Family Tree Builder 4.0 is that it is offered for download completely free of charge.

Family Tree Builder 4.0 claims to be the most popular free family tree building software on the Internet. No1Reviews.com gives accolades to this software that has been downloaded by almost six million users for its ease of use and offered features.

Ease of Use and Navigation

Family Tree Builder 4.0 offers a number of great basic features free of charge, though it provides more advanced features for a premium membership fee. Free users still have access to most of the features one would need to create and manage a family tree. Users can create a family tree simply by adding new individuals and the rest is done by the software. This software is extremely functional, allowing users to visually create their family tree, adding thousands of people with just simple clicks.

Photos and Media

Adding new photos to your family tree is based on a template system. With a few clicks and a photo, you can create a rich, media filled family tree that is a pleasure to navigate and use.

Charts and Reports

As an international site, Family Tree Builder 4.0 supports more than thirty-five languages, complete with the capacity to produce charts in two or more languages and spell check in any one of the supported languages.

Advanced Features

The paid premium membership includes subscription to a family research site, all in one chart (that combine a regular family tree with data sections to make the whole chart a little more exciting), the publishing of videos and documents online, the publishing of your family tree (up to 2,500 names) online on your own dedicated family site, and much more. The SmartMatch feature allows users to automatically match sections of their family trees with those of other users to extend their research. SmartResearch techniques also allow users to automatically research their family trees online on some of the best genealogy sites online.

Legacy Family Tree 7.0 General Information

Legacy Family Tree 7.0 is the newest software package of the successful Legacy Family Tree group, which allows users to build rich, high-quality family trees, and genetic charts using a range of advanced tools. Legacy Family Tree 7.0 is a great site that offers two types of membership options—a free download which opens up access to Legacy Family Tree's most important basic features, and a deluxe download (or CD-ROM) option which provides access to all of Legacy Family Tree's advanced features. Legacy Family Tree 7.0 is affiliated to FamilySearch.org, a genealogy research Web site that works ideally with Legacy Family Tree 7.0. However, although the advanced Family Search integrated function is not ready yet (it is still in production). When it's all ready to go, it will be included in the free standard download package.

Legacy Family Tree 7.0 is fully packed with useful features that will make creating your family tree so much easier. While the deluxe version does open up access to a wide range of premium features, even the standard version provides the average user with all they would need to create a perfect family tree. It's simple to expand your family tree using the standardization templates that are available with the standard version of Legacy Family Tree 7.0. Using these templates is an excellent way to ensure that your family tree is well constructed and contains all the information that you have gleaned from your research.

Advanced Features

No1Reviews.com was impressed with the inclusion of the Legacy SourceWriter, which helps users properly source and cite their research (to genealogy industry standards), regardless of their level of experience. The SourceWriter also produces automatic bibliographies, footnotes, endnotes, and more to make sure that your research is both functionally and visually professional.

Legacy Family Tree 7.0 also has a wide range of other advanced features that are available to those who upgrade to the deluxe version of the software. Deluxe users can make use of Microsoft Visual Earth to view maps of their ancestors' migration, and view 3D and satellite images of their ancestors' key geographical locations. The Interview Centre makes the task of interviewing your family much easier by providing users with a range of prewritten questions and memory prompts. No1Reviews.com was also impressed by the wide range of educational materials that are available from the Web site at no additional cost. The high quality DVD tutorials and glossy booklets ensure that those users who are less confident with the program can still get great results. Although these are only available for an additional fee, No1Reviews.com believes that the fees charged are reasonable, considering the support they provide for its users.

As discussed earlier, the Family Tree Maker software is my personal favorite. As the family historian, I like that the Family Tree Maker makes it easy to build your family tree. Once I entered information in the family tree, in just a few simple steps I was able to upload the information to both Ancestry.com's database of family trees and myfamily.com, the host Web site for our family. We will go into greater detail later in this book with regards to the features of private family Web site. Additionally, Family Tree Maker has provided tools that make it easy for you to organize family photos and other important documents. For those of you who are not interested in creating a private Web site for family, then I would recommend that you upload recorded oral histories, including videos and audio clips, and photos to whatever genealogy software that you decide to use to get organized. On the other hand, if you do opt to create a Web site for your family, you can upload photos, videos, family documents on the Web site, so that this information can be shared with other family members online.

Now you might ask, why should I input my family tree information into genealogy software if I will be creating a Web site for my family? The answer is simple; you need to have a several backup copy of your family tree. Backup copies of your family should be done on CD and online via your family's Web site, as well as being saved on your computer's hard drive. For me, it was many years before I created the Web site for my family but I was still able to enter information into the family tree using the Family Tree Maker software. In fact, I had created the Web site for our family in July of 2010, the week of our family reunion. I was pleasantly surprised to learn the older version of Family Tree Maker that I had was still able to be uploaded to myfamily.com. This is a unique feature of myfamily.com that prevented me from having to enter all of the family tree information for a second time. After you have decided on which genealogy software best suites your family's needs, you then will have the necessary organizational tools available to start your genealogy research.

Chapter 4

Family History Research—Data Collection Phase

Oral History

(Source: http://www.genealogy.com/2_oralhs.html)

Why Is Oral History Important?

Once you have procured your family history documents and started inputting this data in genealogy software, it is time to talk to relatives. Oral histories are stories that living individuals tell about their past, or about the past of other people. Preserving oral history is an important part of genealogy research. Since those who generally provide the information are generally older members of the family, both their lives and their memories are at risk of being lost if you skip this vital step in your family history research. Therefore, it should always be the priority of the family historian to find these patriarchs and matriarchs of the family, whether it be grandparents, great-grandparents, granduncles, grandaunts, great-granduncles, great-grandaunts, older first and second cousins, and even older neighbors and acquaintances of family (Source: http://www.genealogy.com/2_oralhs.html).

What Oral History Can Reveal

You should treat the information you obtain through oral histories as guidance, but not as the ultimate sources, because memories often fade and facts get confused with other facts. Sometimes, however, the information you obtain through oral interviews exists nowhere else and must be taken at face value. Of important value are the stories, anecdotes, family traditions, songs, documents, and especially information associated with pictures, and documents (Source: http://www.genealogy.com/2_oralhs.html).

Oral History Interview

The oral history interview is a method of data collection of your family's history through personal interview. Oral histories are stories that living individuals tell about their past, or about the past of other people. The information gathered through the oral history can be very important in your genealogical research. Typically, you can obtain information on names and places of residence of various family members. You can learn of the places of birth and death, as well as other pertinent information regarding your family. The oral history often involves general storytelling of interesting family events. Oral histories are often an overlooked part of genealogy research that can help us to learn about the people our ancestors were and the times they lived in. It should be incorporated in your family's genealogy research.

Types of Oral History Interviews—Written Records, Audio, and Video

There are several methods that can be used to collect oral histories that include written records, audio tape, and video recordings. When considering individuals to interview you can choose family or close friends, but it's best to start out by interviewing older relatives first since they usually have a wealth of information to share. Of the three methods for obtaining oral history interviews, I recommend that you use written records in addition to audio tape recordings or video. Your written records can be utilized as a backup if you have equipment failure. As part of the preparation process, you should make sure whatever equipment you use works properly, and that you are familiar with its use before the interview (Source: Researching family history: A workbook by Alex J. Helsley. South Carolina Department of Archives and History—Public Program Division).

Interview Location

Whatever setting or location that you choose to conduct your interview, you should make sure that it is quiet and will be free from interference from outside listeners and noise. Nothing is worse than having some type of interruption in the middle of the interview and having to repeat a portion of the interview again. This can make the interview a tiring and frustrating experience.

Preparing for the Interview

(Source: Researching family history: A workbook by Alex J. Helsley. South Carolina Department of Archives and History—Public Program Division)

Before interviewing family members, there are some basic things that you should do to prepare. First, decide on who you will interview and schedule a meeting during a mutually convenient time that will be free of distractions. Second, compile background information on the interviewee and his or her family tree. Third, you should decide upon the focus of the interview. The focus of the interview can be to obtain information about a particular branch of the family, discovering family traditions or customs, or the impact of major historical events (such as war, integration, the Great

Depression, etc.) upon the family. Next, you should prepare a list of questions ahead of time which will serve to facilitate the interview process (see appendix A for list of common interview questions). An often overlooked step is to make sure you have a release form ready to be signed by the interviewee before the interview begins. This will help you to avoid future copyright issues of who may interview. Finally, the purpose of the interview and the equipment to be used should be explained to the interviewee to avoid any confusion about the interview. Please make sure the interviewee is comfortable with your chosen method of interview. Some people may be more comfortable with audio tape recording than video. In the next section, we will discuss the various methods of obtaining an oral history (Source: http://www.marple.com/whyoral.html).

Interviewing Techniques and Guidelines

(Source: Researching family history: A workbook by Alex J. Helsley. South Carolina Department of Archives and History—Public Program Division)

The success of your interview depends on a few but crucial techniques and guidelines that should be followed. These strategies can be considered proper interview etiquette. An important point to mention is that the interviewer should avoid asking closed-ended questions that elicit yes or no answers. The purpose of the interview is to obtain very specific information about your family's history. One way to avoid asking closed-ended questions is to follow a prepared list of questions as discussed earlier. The interviewer should also avoid dominating the conversation. This is not the time to demonstrate how much you know about the interviewee or their family tree. Along with this, the interviewer should avoid interrupting the interviewee. This can convey an attitude of rudeness and may lead to an abbreviated interview. Similarly, the interviewer must be polite and not argue with the interviewee for previously mentioned reason. Additionally, questions should be asked one at a time allowing the interviewee ample time to respond. To validate the information that is shared, it is always a good idea to ascertain how the interviewee acquired the information. This will be helpful to sort out facts from hearsay. One way to confirm the information acquired by the interviewee is to use photographs and other documents as a memory-jogging aid. Discussing landmarks and events is another method of validation. Most people know where they were or what they were doing, let's say, when Dr. Martin Luther King Jr. was assassinated. Moreover, the length of the interview should never extend beyond two hours for obvious reasons such as fatigue, attention span, and possibly boredom. Finally, after the interview is complete, it would be inappropriate to rush off. Just as it is rude to as they say "eat and run" the same applies to oral interview. To display an attitude of appreciation and common courtesy, you should stay for some time after the interview but not long enough to wear out your welcome. You can easily take cues from your host regarding this matter.

Video Interviewing

(Source: http://desktopvideo.about.com/od/homevideoprojects/ht/video-interview.htm)

Again, prepare yourself and your subject for the video interview by talking about the information that you're going to cover and the questions that you're going to ask. Your subject will be more relaxed and the video interview will go more smoothly if you've talked it out ahead of time. Find a good backdrop for conducting the video interview. Ideally, you'll have a location that illustrates something about the person you are interviewing, such as their home. Make sure that the background is attractive and not too cluttered. If you can't find a suitable backdrop for the video interview, you can always seat your subject in front of a blank wall.

Depending on the location of your video interview, you may want to set up some lights. A basic three-point lighting setup can really enhance the look of your video interview. If you're working without a light kit, just use whatever lamps are available to adjust the lighting. Make sure that your subject's face is brightly lit, without any odd shadows.

Set up your video camera on a tripod at eyelevel with your interview subject. The camera should only be three or four-feet from the subject. That way, the interview will be more like a conversation and less like an interrogation.

Use the camera's eyepiece or viewfinder to check the exposure and lighting of the scene. Practice framing your subjects in a wide shot, medium shot, and close-up, and make sure that everything in the frame looks right. Ideally, you'll have a wireless microphone for recording the video interview. Be sure to clip the microphone to the shirt of your interviewee, so that it's out of the way but provides clear audio.

How Can Oral Histories Be Used?

Oral histories provide useful information in helping you to narrow down your search of the family history. It can confirm the accuracy of various sources of information that you have collected such as birth certificates, marriage licenses, and death certificates. These documents will confirm or disprove the information obtained from your oral history.

Genealogy Databases

After you have collected all of your family's resources and interviewed key family members, you are now ready to delve into researching your family's history by utilizing online genealogy databases. Contained in these genealogy databases are records necessary for your research, including, but not limited to, census, vital (birth, marriage, and death), wills and probate, immigration and travel, school, directories, church histories, newspaper, social security indexes, historical documents, and oral history collections, just to name a few. All of these records will help you put the pieces of your family's history together.

As mentioned previously, up to this point, there still will be quite a few missing blanks with regards to your family's history that genealogy databases and records will fill. It doesn't matter which country, city, or state your descendants are from, online genealogy research is the fastest, easiest, most cost-efficient way to discover your roots. When you're researching genealogy records, very seldom can you expect to find all of the information that you need all from a single source. Therefore, the best way to get the most accurate and complete information is to do a combination of searches that covers many different types of genealogy records.

While there are a number of online genealogy databases to choose from, most allow access to the same records for a fee. There are also free online genealogy databases but these sources are not as comprehensive and have limited records you can access. However, before we move on to our discussion of genealogy databases and records, we should define genealogy so that you have an understanding of the process you are about to embark on.

Genealogy is the study of families and the tracing of their lineages and history (Source: http://en.wikipedia.org/wiki/Genealogy). While genealogical research has been prominent for a number of years, in recent years, there has been a substantial increase in the number of individuals turning to the Internet to help them in their research. Online genealogy databases and records serve two main functions. First, they provide access to a wide range of genealogical resources gathered in one place. Second, online genealogy databases allow researchers to generate, then store (online) family trees that are created from researched information. The best part about all of this is that a host of genealogy records can now be accessed online without ever leaving your house. We will begin our discussion of the three most popular genealogy databases according to reviews conducted by No1Reviews.com and to include Ancestry.com, Genealogy.com, and WorldVitalRecord.com (Source: http://genealogy-websites.no1reviews.com/buying-guide.html). If you desire a more global listing of genealogy databases, I will refer you to the Web site Genealogylinks.net. This Web site consists of 4,500 pages of more than 50,000 free genealogy links for the United States, the United Kingdom, England, Scotland, Wales, Ireland, Europe, Canada, Australia, and New Zealand. The types of records you can find using Genealogylinks.net includes parish registers, censuses, cemeteries, marriages, passenger lists, city directories, military records, obituaries, and much more (Source: http://genealogylinks.net/index.html). Now to the number one rated genealogy database,

Ancestry.com (Source: http://genealogy-websites.no1reviews.com/buying-guide.html).

Ancestry.com

(Source: http://genealogy-websites.no1reviews.com/buying-guide.html).

Ancestry.com won the No. 1 Choice Award in the Genealogy Site category. It has the world's only online collection of all publicly available U.S. censuses (1790-1930) digitized and indexed with more than 540 million names included. Ancestry.com's site indicates that they have more than 4 billion individuals from all over the world contained in a vast collection of entries and records from a number of sources. Also, Ancestry.com has the largest collection of international records in the world. In terms of the sheer volume of information, Ancestry.com cannot be beaten, and is the leader in the field of genealogy databases.

Cost

Ancestry.com offers a free fourteen-day trial so that you can decide for yourself if the site is right for you. After the trial period, there are three basic memberships that you can purchase, U.S. Deluxe and World. The U.S. Deluxe membership is $12.95/month, $16.95/month, and $19.95/month respectively for the annual, three-month, and monthly memberships. On the other hand, the World Membership cost is $24.95/month for annual; $27.95/month for the three-month, and $29.95/month for the monthly memberships. Full World Deluxe memberships provides access to billions of record entries from the United States, the United Kingdom, Ireland, Canada, and even further abroad.

Features

Ancestry.com has a vast range of information and document collections to assist your genealogy research. There is the complete U S, U K, Irish, and Canadian census records; voter records; birth, marriage, and death certification (SSDI); military, immigration, and emigration records; card catalogs, public member trees; and OneTreeWorld data. Ancestry.com also includes complete access to specialist record collections, such as Jewish and African American family listings and U.S. yearbook collections from a number of locations dating from the 1930s to 1970s. Moreover, this site includes a huge collection of newspaper articles, obituaries, photos, and family stories to enrich the whole research experience.

Genealogy.com

(Source: http://genealogy-websites.no1reviews.com/buying-guide.html).

Genealogy.com took fourth place after Ancestry.com uk and Ancestry.com au,. according to No.1 Choice Award in their Genealogy site category. With more than 170 million names in its databank and more than 250,000 new records added each week, this site has a lot to offer.

Cost

Genealogy.com also offers a free fourteen-day trial to try out their database and afterward there are three levels of subscriptions including Basic ($69.99 annually), Deluxe ($99.99 annually), and Gold Membership ($199.99 annually).

Features

The membership options available on Genealogy.com differ in

terms of their information provision and access to records. Basic membership opens up access to the genealogy library with access to a number of U.S. records (birth, marriage, and death statistics and military records), while the Deluxe membership includes access to World Family Tree, too. Gold membership includes access to complete U.S. Census information and information from passenger immigration records. This membership provides access to the most useful information, and includes free complete technical support.

WorldVitalRecords.com

(Source: http://genealogy-websites.no1reviews.com/buying-guide.html).

World Vital Records.com was next in standing of U.S. genealogy online databases as rated by No.1 Choice Award in their Genealogy site category.

Cost

WorldVitalRecords.com offers two major membership options and offers only a seven-day free trial. The cost of membership differs as follows: US Collection ($3.33/month for annual and $5.95/month) and World Collection ($9.95/month for annual and $14.95/month).

Features

The membership options available on WorldVitalRecords offers two membership options, membership to the U.S. Collection provides unlimited access to all the U.S.record collections (immigration lists, census records, vital records, and parish and land records) and access to more than 800 million U.S. ancestral names. The World Collection membership offers all of the benefits of U.S. Collection Membership, plus Access to more than 1.2 billion ancestral names, and unlimited access to all records from the United Kingdom, Ireland, Canada, and more.

Genealogy Records

After reviewing the most popular genealogy databases and the features they offer, we should now explore in detail the various types of records contained in them. These records include census, vital records (birth, marriage, and death), and wills and probate. Some of the less researched records include, but not limited to, immigration and travel, newspaper articles and obituaries, and social security death indexes. Finally, to include school directories, church histories, and various other historical documents.

Census Records

(Source: http://search.ancestry.com/search, http://genealogistrecords.com, http://wilson.lib.umn.edu/reference/gen-how.html#census and http://en.wikipedia.org/wiki/National_Archives_and_Records Administration).

Census records are the cornerstone of family history research and for tracking your relatives. The federal census of the U.S. population, mandated by the U.S. Constitution, has been taken every ten years since 1790. These records can provide information about your ancestors' residences, birthplace, immigration, occupation, education level, and socioeconomic status. Census sheet is organized by listing the head of household and other family members with their ages. Some records even contain information on immigration, citizenship, military service, and more. Census records can help you to pinpoint the locations of family members within a state or county and to obtain information about other family members.

While census records can provide valuable information about your family's history and is a good starting point for your genealogy research, there are some drawbacks you should keep in mind such as inconsistent, inaccurate, and omitted information. Also, you will learn that there were periods of time where a number of census records were destroyed.

Although the census has been taken of the U.S. population every ten years since 1790, however, only the census from 1790 to 1930 is available to search, since it is the law that individual census is sealed for seventy-two years due to mandated privacy restriction. Once you begin your research, you will find that the questions and information contained on census records varies from decade to decade, and from state to state. For example, from 1790 to 1840, the only information requested on the censuses was the name of the head of the household and the number of family members between certain ages. Beginning with the 1850 census, other family members are listed by name and age with occupations given. Some subsequent censuses list where the individual was born, his or her parents were born, the number of years of education, and even whether the individual owned or rented property.

Besides finding inconsistent information, several censuses have been lost or destroyed. Most notably, much of the 1790 census was destroyed during the War of 1812. Likewise, the 1890 census was almost totally destroyed by fire and water damage.

Don't be surprised to find inaccuracies from one census to

another since the census information was only as reliable as the person obtaining the information. Census takers were often poorly trained. They may have left families off the census due to human error and frank omissions. A common problem that I encountered was differences in the spelling of names and sometimes nicknames being used rather than real names. I often found inconsistencies in the ages of various family members from census to census. Despite its problems, the census contains invaluable information that should not be overlooked.

Now that good understanding of what you will find on the census records, let's begin to explore how to best research census reports. As has already been mentioned, I began my research of my family's history over twenty years ago. At that time, the availability of online census records and databases were essentially nonexistent, so I had to visit the National Archives building. Fortunately for me, I lived close to the National Archives in Philadelphia, PA. The Philadelphia National Archives is an affiliated branch of The National Archives and Records Administration (NARA) which is an independent agency of the U.S. government charged with preserving and documenting government and historical records and with increasing public access to those documents, which comprise the National Archives. Part of NARA's collection of historical records includes the census from 1790 to 1930, as well as ships passenger lists and naturalization records. My trips to the National Archives involved viewing census records on microfilm at this time. What a tedious process but rewarding process at the end. In my research, I was able to obtain information about by great-great-grandfather and his family from the 1860 South Carolina census. I discovered what town he in lived in, number and names of household members, their ages, and occupations. I can't begin to tell you what a very exciting and emotional experience this was for me having made this discovery. The nice part about this was that I was able to build on the information I found on the 1860 census from subsequent census records. All three aforementioned genealogy databases—Ancestry.com, Genealogy.com, and WorldVitalRecords.com offer access to census data.

Vital Records—Birth, Marriage, and Death

(Source: http://search.ancestry.com/search and http://wilson.lib.umn.edu/reference/gen-how.html#census)

The recording of vital records—births, marriages, and deaths was started in 1837 and is one of the most significant resources for genealogical research. The transcribing of the records is carried out by teams of dedicated volunteers and contains index information for the period 1837-1983.

I would recommend researching the vital records section of the government ancestry files. All of the records that are kept in the various divisions come from individual encounters with the government though the lifespan. From the time you are born until the day that you die, you interact with the government several times. Ancestry.com, Genealogy.com, and WorldVitalRecords.com, all provide online access to vital records.

For those of you who are not proficient in doing your research online or don't have access to a computer, you can request vital records from every state. Each state has a Department of Vital Statistics from which these records can be obtained for a small fee. For example, death certificates contain information such as year and place of birth, date and city of death, cause of death, and names of parents. This is important information in conducting your genealogical research.

Wills and Probate Records

(Source: http://dohistory.org/on_your_own/toolkit/probateRecords.html)

Wills and probate records can provide you with all sorts of fascinating information, Probate records are those kept by a probate court. The word probate comes from Latin and means "to prove," in this case to prove in court the authenticity of a last will and testament of someone who has died. In the absence of a will, inheritance laws have provided for the passing on of property, belongings, and assets.

Probate courts are under state jurisdiction. State probate laws have changed over the centuries. The kinds of records to be found in probate files have changed accordingly. Probate laws can vary from state to state but tend to follow certain general practices. The probate of the estate of someone who has died and has left a will is called testate. The probate of the estate of someone who has died but has not left a will is called intestate.

Probate records can usually be found in the court records of the county where the deceased was last living. In some cases, early records have been moved to other depositories such as state archives, to allow for better security, temperature and humidity control, and more space for newer records. As storage space and available facilities change, so do the sites of probate records. The documents found in a probate file will vary radically. They may range from a single letter to a sheaf of court and family documents.

Probate records can give the historian invaluable information. For example, genealogists value the lists of heirs and devisees that indicate familial relationships. People researching material culture can learn much from household inventories. Historians trying to learn more about particular buildings often find useful information in real estate inventories.

Probate Research

There are some basic steps you should take in the process of searching through probate records. First, determine where the deceased was living at time of death. Then find out where the records for that probate court jurisdiction at that time are now housed. Remember that the boundaries and names of counties might have changed. If this is the case, and the county (or state) has changed, then the records will be filed with the records in the county at the time of death, not under the county's name as it is now. You will save yourself steps by using the Internet and the telephone to ask for and find the archive that you want. Many states and counties have Web sites. Next, find the index of the probate records you want. This will be at the archive that holds the probate records. It's best to look online for a Web site of the likely archive. Today, many archives now have Web home pages with holdings information. The probate index you want might even become accessible online. To search for online probate records by county USGenWeb Archives' virtual courthouse allows you to do a search by state then county for online wills and probate records (Source: www.rootsweb.com/usgenweb). For links to multiple probate and wills sites, refer to Cyndi's List of sites pertaining to wills and probates at www.CyndisList.com/wills.htm. Also through Ancestry.com you can access online wills and other probate records.

For those of you who don't have access to computer will need to go to the archive. Look in the index for the deceased's name. This will usually be listed alphabetically by surname. Find and note the docket number. Usually the date of probate is also listed, and this is usually fairly close to the date of death. Be thorough. Look also under the names of relatives of the deceased—you might be surprised to find a file full of relevant documents. Make a list of files you wish to see and give these to the clerk, who will retrieve the files for you. If the files are old and are in a storage facility off-site, it might take several days for the request to be filled. This is all the more reason to make the request online or by telephone if you can. If files are missing, and they sometimes are, probate record books might give some evidence of the probate. Probate record books are not likely to contain all the information that is/was in the actual file, however. Examine the files and make notes. The cost of making photocopies will vary from archive to archive. It may be as little as 15 cents per page to a dollar or more per page. Return the original file, as you found it, to the clerk. Label and file your findings, being sure to note the name of the archive, address, telephone number, Web site address, and the date you did your research there.

Immigration and Travel Records

The records in this collection document the journey of your immigrant ancestors and their steps toward becoming a citizen of their new country. They include passenger arrival records, naturalization records, border crossings, emigration records, passports, and convict transportation records. The collection includes immigration records from the United States and several other countries from around the world. Ancestry.com likely has the largest collection of immigration and travel records available online.

Schools, Directories and Church Histories

Directories and member lists typically contain the name of the person and address, and in the case of city directories you will also learn their occupation. These records are helpful in placing your ancestor in a specific location in a particular year. Other collections in this category include church histories, church records, alumni list, yearbooks, professional directories, and phone books. Once again, Ancestry.com likely has the largest collection of information on school records, directories, and church histories available online.

Newspaper Databanks

(Source: http://www.genealogybank.com/gbnk)

GenealogyBank.com exclusive database has the largest newspaper archive for family history research. This Web site provides information on millions of American families from 1690 to this day. Over 4,400 newspapers provide firsthand accounts about your ancestors. You'll be amazed by the stories, names, dates, places, and events that have played a role in your family's history.

You can also search newspaper obituaries on GenealogyBank.com. Searching newspaper obituaries is another great place to find information about family. Obituaries contain names, dates, places of birth, marriage, and other helpful family history information.

You also find this information on Ancestry.com's Web site.

Social Security Death Index

(Source: http://www.deathindexes.com/ssdi.html)

The Social Security Death Index (SSDI) is a database of people whose deaths were reported to the Social Security Administration (SSA), beginning about 1962. A small number of deaths were listed before 1962. It was created from the SSA's Death Master File. You will not find everyone who died from 1962 to the present, but it does list many deaths in that time frame, especially in more recent years (particularly from the late 1980s to the present). It is close to being a national death index for the United States. If you find someone listed in the SSDI you can usually order a copy of the form they filled out when they applied for a Social Security Card (SS-5 form) from the SSA for a fee. This record usually has more information about the person such as date and place of birth and names of parents. If your ancestor died before 1962 (or they are deceased, but not in the SSDI) and you believe they may have applied for a Social Security Card, you can still obtain a copy of their SS-5 (you will need to provide proof of death). The first SS-5s were used in late 1936. The SSA does not have information about people who died before about 1940 when social security payments were first paid out. The SSDI has very few entries for people who died from 1940-1961. Try the state listings below for some death indexes before 1962 (and for other time frames).

There are three popular online databases that provide access to the SSDI with over 88 million records for individuals with U S social security numbers. Rootsweb (http://ssdi.rootsweb.ancestry.com/cgi-bin/ssdi.cgi) and GenealogyBank.com (http://www.genealogybank.com/gbnk) provide free access to the up-to-date SSDI. Conversely, Ancestry.com is fee-based that includes access to the SSDI as part of subscription.

Historical Documents

You can find vast number of historical documents on two primary online databases. Military records, casualty lists, revolutionary and civil war pension requests, widow's claims, orphan petitions, land grants, and much more can be accessed on GenealogyBank.com Web site (Source: http://www.genealogybank.com/gbnk).

Ancestry.com houses millions of U.S. military records, covering almost four hundred years of American wars and conflicts from before the Revolutionary War up to Vietnam War. With over 100 million names and seven hundred databases of military records from all fifty U.S. states, there are countless opportunities to learn the stories of courage and sacrifice in your family tree (Source: http://www.ancestry.com/militaryrecords).

Oral History Collections

Transcribed oral history collections may assist researchers who are beginning their genealogies or family histories. There are many such collections in archives and libraries around the United States. They range from interviews of miners, cowboys, Indians, and early settlers, to industrial leaders, politicians, doctors, midwives, ecclesiastical leaders, those in the military, and so forth. Sometimes by speaking with a relative, you'll find that they or another family member has already participated in an oral history project. That means that some of the work has already been done for you, so you can move on to other projects instead of duplicating efforts.

The National Press Club Archives holds two large collections of oral history interviews done by the National Press Club Oral History Committee and by the Washington Press Club Foundation. Some oral histories include audio or video, while others have both. Most of the oral histories conducted by the National Press Club do not have transcripts. All of the oral histories conducted by the Washington Press Club Foundation have transcripts. Researchers and family historians are encouraged to make an appointment with the archivist to listen or view any tapes or transcripts. For a complete list of oral histories, please consult the links below. Note that some oral histories are closed to the public, and they are not authorized to duplicate or release any closed materials (Source: http://press.org/library/archives/oral-histories).

The Archives and Modern Manuscript's Oral History Collections cover a broad range of topics, people, and institutions from throughout the medical and health sciences. Chiefly from the 1960s to the present, the collections consist of interviews with physicians, scientists, government administrators, medical librarians, and health-business executives. AMMP is also the service home for the Food and Drug Administration and the Medical Library Association oral history programs. This content is also available online and organized into two collections, which include digitized transcripts plus any accompanying audio content when feasible. Users can browse content by title, interviewee name, and subject. Full-text searching is available across all sub collections, across each sub-collection, and within each transcript. New collections are added over time (Source: http://www.nlm.nih.gov/hmd/manuscripts/oh.html).

Genetic Genealogy and DNA Testing

There is a new science available now for genealogists around the world enabling them to advance their family's research. Genetic genealogy is the newest and most exciting addition to genealogy research. Now individuals can discover their ancestry roots, including where ancestors came from, their ethnic background, and trace the source of their surname. This can all be done by obtaining a simple DNA test.

Most of us are probably familiar with the use of DNA testing in solving crimes and confirming paternity. However, only in recent years that we have learned how DNA testing can be used in the discovery of a family's ancient origins. Whether our ancestors migrated out of Africa, Europe, or other lands, DNA testing can trace a family's roots.

Genetic Genealogy and DNA testing have become popular as well in recent years. This is demonstrated by increased media attention and coverage of TV programs relating to the discovery of one's ancestry. You now see television commercials sponsored by Ancestry.com encouraging Americans to discover their roots by joining their Web site. Ancestry.com has spent millions of dollars to increase the public's awareness of genealogy.

The new prime-time television shows on NBC, "Who Do You Think You Are?" is now in its second season. This unique, award-winning series takes an up-close and personal look each week of some of America's best-known celebrities as they are taken on a quest of discovering their family's history. Celebrities such as Rosie O'Donnell, Vanessa Williams, Lisa Kudrow, and Sarah Jessica Parker, just to name a few, have been featured over the past two seasons. This journey is one of suspense, intrigue, and deeply emotional encounters. Stories are uncovered of heroism, tragedies, love, betrayal, and long-held secrets that lie at the heart of these celebrities' family history (Source: http://www.nbc.com/who-do-you-think-you-are/about). So, let's explore this new science in detail.

The Science of DNA Testing

(Source: African Ancestry Guide to West and Central Africa. African Ancestry Inc., Washington, DC, 2008)

DNA is found in the cells of our body and contains all the information necessary to coordinate the functions of our body. DNA tells us important information about our maternal and paternal genetic ancestries. We receive half of the DNA in our body from our mother and the other half from our father. Because of this, we can go back many generations to determine the percentage of DNA we have received from our ancestors. There are two types of DNA known as mitochondrial (mtDNA) and Y-chromosome DNA (NRY) that define the maternal and paternal lineages. Also, these two types of DNA can provide you with information that is geographically and regionally specific.

Procedure for DNA Test Sample Collection

The process involved in collecting the DNA test sample is quite simple. DNA test sample is obtained by swabbing the inside of your mouth to collect cheek cells. Genetic markers are then sequenced or genotyped. These markers are then compared to a database of genetic lineage identifying specific populations. Usually the test results can be obtained in time frames from about four to six weeks.

Chapter 5

Preserving the Family History and Sharing

Why Is Sharing and Preserving Family History Important?

Preserving and sharing your family's history is an important part of genealogical research and data preservation and for some very good reasons. Most of the benefits of knowing one's family history have already been discussed in chapter 1. Sharing family history can be vital information for future generations. We learned that sharing one's family history creates a legacy for future generations. The legacy of our ancestors, whether good or bad, grounds and shapes us as individuals, and also provides us with a greater sense of identity. Moreover, by sharing our family's history, we provide a tangible connection to the past. History is the only link between you and those of a distant generation. This gives each of us a place in the family structure and explains where we came from, how we fit in, and how the family has grown and changed over time (Source: http://www.howtofindyourroots.com/).

A benefit not discussed previously is that sharing your family's happiest memories and experiences with others can be fun and gratifying. It is amazing how much we don't know about our own family and how interesting the information we learn can be to us (Source: http://www.howtofindyourroots.com/).

The process of preserving the family's history is generally the responsibility of the family historian. However, anyone who shares an interest in preserving the family's history can participate. Whoever, decides to participate in preserving the family's history must understand that it is an ongoing process that never really ever ends.

There are many ways to preserve your family memories and history, using family history books, PowerPoint presentations, family tree poster, digital photo scrapbook, DVD movies, and creating private family Web site. With the technological advances today, there are many computer programs available that will help you to preserve and share your family's history in a number of creative ways. We will now begin explore some of these creative ways starting with a discussion of the family history book.

Family History Book

Now that you've worked hard to discover your family's history, and you want to preserve your research in a form that will stand the test of time—a Family History Book that can be shared today as well as archived for future generations.

Steps in Writing Your Family History Book

(Source: http://genealogy.about.com/od/writing_family_history/a/write.htm)

Decide on the Type of Book to Create The first decision you must make is the type of book you would like to create. A simple photocopied booklet shared only with family members or a full-scale, hard-bound book to serve as a reference for other genealogists.

While there is no one ideal way to present all of your genealogy material, the most efficient and logical way for most people is in a book based on the genealogy format report, that is the register format (used by the New England Historic Genealogical Register) and National Genealogical Society record format (used by the NGS Quarterly). These formats number people logically, arrange them by generation, allow for the use of footnotes, and accommodate additional text on individuals where you can tell their stories. These forms start with the oldest ancestor and include all descendants. Another form based on the Ahnentafel System starts with the youngest person and includes all the ancestors and ancestor's siblings of that individual. These formats also use the least amount of paper (Source:http://www.genealogy.com/21_prze.html).

However, if you want to simplify the process of book writing, I recommend using a genealogy software programs. These programs can help with the time-consuming tasks, such as numbering the entries and creating an index to every surname. The best programs on the market allow you to make your book more interesting with photos, graphics, captions, and a wide variety of beautiful charts and trees (Source: http://genealogy.about.com/library/reviewaatpgen_publishing.htm). Top picks once again in this area are Family Tree Maker 2011, Legacy Family Tree Deluxe 6.0, and Roots Magic, according to TopTenReviews (Source: http://genealogy-software-review.toptenreviews.com/). Family Tree Maker 2011s publishing program is integrated with Ancestry.com, allowing Ancestry's members to automatically create family history books based on data, records, and photos in their online trees. MyCanvas offers premium Family History Books available in 11" × 8.5" format with a velvet or nubuck cover. Premium photo books are available in

11" × 8.5" or 8" × 8" with four cover types: velvet, nubuck, genuine leather, or Japanese silk.

With all of these genealogy software programs, simplify the process of book writing through the auto-fill feature with your saved information. You can also choose to build your own book from scratch.

Define the Scope of Your Family History Book

(Source: http://genealogy.about.com/od/writing_family_history/a/write.htm)

The next decision you must make is to define the scope of your book. Do you intend to write mostly about one particular relative, or everyone hanging from your family tree? Whether you write about one relative or many, you must choose the focus of the book: single line of descent, all descendants, or a particular generation.

Single Line of Descent

If the single line of descent is your focus, begin with the earliest known ancestor for a particular surname and follow him/her through a single line of descent (to yourself, for example). Each chapter of your book would cover one ancestor or generation.

All Descendants

On the other hand, if all descendants are your focus, start with an individual or couple and cover all of their descendants, with chapters organized by generation. Keep in mind, these suggestions can easily be adapted to fit your interests, time, and creativity.

Establish Attainable Deadlines

http://genealogy.about.com/od/writing_family_history/a/write.htm

Deadlines disciplines you, helps you to stay on track to complete your book. This is not to say that you will be challenged to complete your book. Your objective is to breakdown various sections of book into specified time frames. For example, you may set of goal of one month to complete each chapter or section of your book. Another suggestion for meeting deadlines is to schedule writing time each day. You can decide whether what works best for you based on your life. You'll be surprised what you can accomplish in a few hours a day.

Choose a Plot or Theme

(Source: http://genealogy.about.com/od/writing_family_history/a/write.htm)

A plot or theme gives your Family History Book interest and focus. Popular family history plots and themes include stories of immigration/migration, rags to riches, pioneer or farm life, rise out of slavery, or war survival. When considering a plot or theme, think of your ancestors as characters in your family history book. It's helpful if you research some of the problems and obstacles your ancestors faced. You should attempt to capture the most interesting parts of your family's history. For example, did your ancestors escape a life of poverty and persecution for a better one in a new country? Were any of your ancestors' inventors or have an unusual occupation? Consider writing about wartime heroes. You can choose from any of these themes or plots to write your family's story. If you have an interesting story, you will be able to grab your reader's attention, with the hope of drawing them in past in the first page. You can later use flashback to fill in the reader on the events which lead up to your opening story.

Be Creative

If you want your family history to read more like a suspense novel than a dull, dry textbook, then it is important to make the reader feel like an eyewitness to your family's life. Even if your ancestors did not leave an account of his or her daily life, social histories can help you learn about the experiences of people in a given time and place. One way to do this is to read town and city histories to learn what life was like during your time period of interest. Investigate your ancestor's occupation to gain greater understanding into his daily activities. This can easily be found in census records. If you haven't already, be sure to interview all of your living relatives. Family stories told in a relative's own words will add a personal touch to your book.

Make it Personal

(Source: http://genealogy.about.com/od/writing_family_history/a/write.htm)

Those individuals reading your book will likely be interested in the facts, but what they'll most enjoy and remember are the everyday details—favorite stories and anecdotes, embarrassing moments and family traditions. There are times when it can be interesting to include varying accounts of the same event. However, personal stories offer a great way to introduce new characters and chapters, and keep your reader interested. In the instance that your ancestors did not leave any personal accounts, you can still tell their story as if they had, using what you've learned about them from your research.

With the addition of photos, pedigree charts, maps, and other illustrations, your book can have added interest to your family history, by breaking up the writing into manageable sections for the reader. Be sure not to leave out detailed captions for any photos or illustrations that you include.

PowerPoint Presentation of the Family History

(Source: http://123genealogy.com/shopping/product_details.php?id=11 and http://www.ancestry.com/learn/library/article.aspx?article=4204

After spending countless hours researching my family's history, the most exciting part for me was to have an opportunity to present this information at the family reunion. In 1993, at our first national family reunion, I had photos converted into slides that I used as I gave a narrative of my family's history. This presentation was impressive at the time since many individuals that I had spoken with at venues such as The Family Reunion Conference sponsored by Temple University Family Reunion Institute and the African American Genealogy Group meetings usually included their family's history in the Reunion Souvenir Book. Today, there are several ways in which to create an impressive PowerPoint presentation of your family's history that I would like to discuss. If you have Microsoft PowerPoint software loaded on your computer, you can create you project from scratch. However, there is software comes with hundreds of colorful PowerPoint backgrounds in a variety of font styles and images that you can customize to your preference.

Microsoft PowerPoint 2010

(Source: http://office.microsoft.com/en-us/powerpoint/powerpoint-2010-features-and-benefits-HA101809930.aspx)

Microsoft PowerPoint 2010 gives you more ways to create and share dynamic presentations with your family. It offers exciting new audio and visual capabilities that help you tell a crisp, cinematic story that's as easy to create as it is powerful to watch. Additionally, PowerPoint2010 enables you to work simultaneously with other people or post your presentation online and access it from virtually anywhere using the Internet or your smart phone. PowerPoint is a very user-friendly program and you can insert photos from other files with ease. Once you get the hang of it, adding the captions are easy. You will be surprised as to how much genealogy information you can get into those captions.

Steps in Creating a PowerPoint Presentation

(Source: http://office.microsoft.com/en-us/powerpoint-help/basic-tasks-in-powerpoint-2010-HA101824346.aspx)

Select a Template

The first step in creating a PowerPoint Presentation is selecting a template. A template is a starting point for presentation. It actually is a file contained on PowerPoint that formats your slides. Templates come in a variety of backgrounds, colors, animations, graphics, font styles, and sizes. PowerPoint 2010 allows you to apply built-in templates to your project. To find a template in PowerPoint 2010, you must follow these steps:

1. On the File tab, click New

2. Under Available Templates and Themes, do one of the following

a. To use one of the built-in templates installed with PowerPoint, click Sample Templates, click the template that you want, and then click Create.

Create a Presentation

1. Click the File tab, and then click New.

2. Click Blank Presentation, and then click Create.

3. Apply a template or theme, either from those built-in with PowerPoint 2010, or downloaded from Office.com. See Find and apply a template in this article.

Open a Presentation

1. Click the File tab, and then click Open.

2. In the left pane of the Open dialog box, click the drive or folder that contains the presentation that you want.

3. In the right pane of the Open dialog box, open the folder that contains the presentation.

4. Click the presentation, and then click Open. By default, PowerPoint 2010 shows only PowerPoint presentations in the Open dialog box. To view other kinds of files, click All PowerPoint

Presentations, and select the type of file that you want to view.

Save a Presentation

1. Click the File tab, and then click Save As.

2. In the File name box, type a name for your PowerPoint presentation, and then click Save. By default, PowerPoint 2010 saves files in the PowerPoint Presentation (.pptx) file format. To save your presentation in a format other than. pptx, click the Save as type list, and then select the file format that you want.

Insert a New Slide

On the Home tab, in the Slides group, click the arrow below New Slide, and then click the slide layout that you want.

Add Shapes to the Slide

1. On the Home tab, in the Drawing group, click Shapes.

2. Click the shape that you want, click anywhere on the slide, and then drag to place the shape. To create a perfect square or circle (or constrain the dimensions of other shapes), press and hold Shift while you drag.

View a Slide Show

1. To view your presentation in Slide Show view from the first slide, on the Slide Show tab, in the Start Slide Show group, click From Beginning.

2. To view your presentation in Slide Show view from the current slide, On the Slide Show tab, in the Start Slide Show group, click From Current Slide.

Print a Presentation

1. Click the File tab, and then click Print.

2. Under "Print What," you should click All to print all slides. To print only the slide that is currently displayed, click Current Slide. If you only want to print specific slides by number, click Custom Range of Slides, and then enter a list of individual slides, a range, or both.

3. Under Other Settings, click the Color list, and select the setting that you want.

4. When you finish making your selections, click Print.

PowerPoint Background CD for Family History Software

For those of you who choose not to create a PowerPoint presentation from scratch, the "PowerPoint Background CD for Family History" produced by 123genealogy.com may be an option for you. This CD currently sells for $9.95 and features 750 colorful PowerPoint backgrounds in a variety of colors and font styles with eighty-four images. You have the capability of being able mix and match colors, images, and font styles to customize your presentation. The backgrounds are simple, consisting mostly of banners along the top, sides, or bottom of each slide. The scanned images include old tombstones, sailing ships, cowboys, old houses, eyeglasses, naturalization certificates, and a variety of people dressed in the fashions of a century ago. These images will add visual interest to your presentation. The CD-ROM also includes a viewer program that you can use to easily browse through the various backgrounds on the disk, choose the ones you like, and then easily import them into PowerPoint. The images are all "softened," that is, they are not razor-sharp pictures. Instead, they are designed to appear as soft background images and will never "overpower" your presentation materials.

Digital Photo Family History Scrapbook

(Source: http://scrapbooking-software-review.toptenreviews.com)

One of the most amazing things that can be created with your family history information is a digital photo family history scrapbook. A family history photo scrapbook is a great way to educate your family, for generations to come, on their past. Scrapbooking is a hobby that's been around for some time. The method of scrapbooking that we are most familiar with involves photo album type requiring materials such as paper, cloth, and other mementos. The materials needed to prepare a scrapbook can be expensive. An alternate to traditional scrapbooking is digital photo scrapbooking made available online or in CD software formats. What took weeks or months to complete now can be done in hours. You can experiment with various colors and design without having to worry about wasting costly scrapbooking supplies. The flexibility of digital scrapbooking gives you what was unheard-of in previous years. Scrapbooking software allows you to select from hundreds of templates to find inspiration for your creation. The price range for the most popular software packages ranges between $28.99 and $49.99.

Preparing for Your Scrapbook

When preparing for your digital scrapbook, items that you should include are photos, newspaper clippings, and any other important family history documents that you desire. Ideally, it's best to own your own flatbed scanner. However, if this is not possible, you can have photos and other documents scanned at your local photo shop.

General Features of Digital Scrapbooking Software

There are three main features you should look for when choosing the appropriate scrapbooking software and includes multimedia importing, offer multiple design features and exporting options in a variety of formats. Without these features, you will not be able to produce a superb finished product.

Multimedia Importing

Any scrapbooking software that you choose should give you several options to import media into your scrapbook creations. The software that you choose must allow you to bring in images, video, and audio without having to wade through a bunch of different menus to get the job done. Generally, you don't have to worry about importing images from your digital camera or scanner because a lot of these programs have import capabilities for both kinds of devices imbedded in them. This cuts down on the time you would spend uploading and reformatting these graphics. Once you have completed your scrapbook page, you can share them with Web albums, online user communities, DVD, video CD, and iPod. Users can also take advantage of new features offered by some software packages, like voice narration, audio, and video.

Design Features

Any scrapbooking software that you choose will provide you with enough design features to create the perfect scrapbook. The basic design features that you should look for in scrapbooking are a word art, embellishments, image effects, and photo editing.

Export Options

The scrapbooking software you choose must have options to export your scrapbook into a number of different formats. Your project isn't going anywhere if all you can do is save it into the file type specific to the program you're using.

Top Rated Digital Scrapbooking Software

(Source: http://scrapbooking-software-review.toptenreviews.com/)

TopTenReviews equips you with the information needed to make the best choice of digital scrapbooking software for 2011. The recommendations given are based on side-by-side comparison charts, news, articles, and videos that simplify the buying process for purchasers. The editors and senior writers are supported by thirty additional staff writers that provide high quality, informational reviews. The staff members of TopTenReviews come from diverse professional backgrounds, each bringing their own area of expertise to the reviews they write. TopTenReviews won a 2010 OMMA Award, recognizing the best of the online media, marketing, and advertising industries, for Web Site Excellence as selected by judges and industry executives. The top three rated software packages have been reviewed by TopTenReviews. A summary of the features is discussed below. examining pros and cons of each. We will look at My Memories Suite, Memory Mixer, and Digital Scrapbook Artist.

My Memories Suite

My Memories Suite has everything you can look for in digital scrapbooking software. TopTenReviews has given My Memories Suite their number one rating. It is ease of use and has nearly unlimited choices in design that allows you to alter practically every template. The capability to download new pages, kits, and embellishments from the design store is a great feature.

Importing

The importing feature that allows you to add is simple. You can import entire album files and have them automatically populate your template pages, or you can just as easily drag and drop individual images right where you want them. We were also able to grab images from the Internet and drop them into albums. This ability makes it simple for you to add images from image hosting sites like Flickr, Photobucket, or even Facebook.

Design Features

Attractive scrapbooking pages can be created in minutes by using My Memories Suite's free or purchased templates. Everything on a page can be edited. For example, you can copy design elements like boxes or flourishes, and they can also be moved around, rotated, and resized. You can even change the color of template elements to create a whole new look. Additionally, you can add paper designs or textures to template items.

With the digital scrapbooking software, you are able to add text boxes as well as create text art with its Word Art Designer. This tool will let you create and save unique text styles. The text tool includes many fonts. The word art tool utilizes the fonts available, but you can also rotate the text, select fill types and opacity, and adjust stroke width and opacity. Shadowing and beveling effects can be added and text can be arranged to display in ways other than a straight line, such as in a downward or upward arc shape.

This scrapbooking software includes numerous embellishments that can be altered, as well as over 30 album templates, 1,500 paper types, and 1,300 page embellishments. You can easily add shapes to pages as well as links, music, or video. A favorite feature of this software is the color editing tool. Not only can you simply just pick a color, but you can also adjust HSB and RGB values or use the Color Picker. The Color Picker will display a preview image of your page and you simply select the color you want to match. The gradient tool was especially fun to play with; after you pick your color, it can be used to create customized gradient color swatches, and you can even adjust the point at which that the color starts and in which direction the color will fade.

My Memories Suite does include some basic photo editing tools as well. You have the capability to resize images, crop images, zoom in and out, and reduce red-eyes. You can also add image effects such as black and white, sepia, mirroring, and emboss. The photo editing tools included with this software are suitable for most basic editing; however, for advanced editing you may want to consider using a professional photo editing application.

Design Shop

The design shop is where the design fun really begins. The free pages and templates that come with the software really are just a teaser compared to what you can get online. And My Memories Suite even offers numerous free downloads. You can also purchase templates, papers, and full packages. They offer over 350 templates and over 500 packs that include emblems, frames, and paper packs, each for under $10. They feature fifteen designers that all have a distinctive style to help create a varied collection for you to choose from. Even if you do not own a copy of My Memories Suite, you can still download and utilize the designs they offer.

Output Options

My Memories Suite includes quite a few sharing options. Of course you can print your creations with your printer, but you can also export them as JPEGs or as an iPod- or iPhone-ready movie. You can also create photo albums, greeting cards, trading cards, and calendars. This digital scrapbooking software can also create videos and burn them to a DVD. My Memories Suite also provides a printing service that can assemble professionally printed and bound photo albums in a variety of sizes. You can choose from hard cover, soft cover, leather bound, and wire-o bound books.

Memory Mixer

Memory Mixer was rated number two by TopTenReviews and offers Web friendly pages for creating fun photo pages, books, and images for the Internet. Memory Mixer posts many sample pages online, so go check them out to get an idea of what you can do with this digital scrapbooking software, you will be surprised.

Importing

Although this software does not support direct uploading from external devices like cell phones or cameras, it can import from any image file, so once your images are uploaded to your computer you can easily add them to your scrapbook pages through the program. You can also copy images from the Internet and directly paste them into a page, which is a great time-saving tool.

Design Features

Memory Mixer provides a variety of backgrounds, papers, embellishments, fonts, and shapes. In terms of backgrounds you can choose a solid color using the provided swatches, alter colors of the existing backgrounds or create your own with the Color Picker. Paper can be altered or created and this software includes a selection of designer packages that make beautiful rush jobs easy to accomplish. You can also choose from a selection of textures, including fabric, metal, and nature textures.

Embellishments include things like corners, ribbons, flowers, leaves, stitching, buttons, letters, frames, and even words and expressions. Of course you can import your own embellishments and graphics and alter them. For example, you can easily resize your objects, rotate them, change their opacity and then add them to your favorites so you can quickly find them later.

Memory Mixer allows you to easily add text and journaling to your layouts. It offers many font types and you can modify the text using any color or opacity that you desire. Select the orientation, size, bold or italic, underline, and even fit the text to a shape. This scrapbooking software offers a diversity of fun shapes that you can add to your designs as well, such as squares, hearts, stars, talk bubbles, and more. Of course you can change the orientation, size, color, and opacity of the shapes.

Output Options

With Memory Mixer you can easily share your pages or albums by burning them to a CD or DVD, by creating a movie, by printing or by converting to a JPEG for sharing on the Internet. You can also have a photobook printed through Memory Mixer for as low as $9.95.

Digital Scrapbook Artist

Digital Scrapbook Artist from Serif has nabbed the number three spot from TopTenReviews for 2011. This program is designed to help the novice and experienced scrapbooked alike to figure out its features and interface on their way to making beautiful scrapbooks. With the new blending and stenciling tools, it has never been easier to turn your project into a beautiful work of art. Digital Scrapbook Artist is an excellent digital scrapbooking software that makes it easy to create digital works of art. It has a wide variety of included high-quality elements and tools including a spell checker and respectable photo editor. It lacks the capability of creating craft-related projects like calendars or tee shirts.

Importing

One of the strong points of Digital Scrapbook Artist is its capability to import images from numerous sources such as a digital camera, scanner, CD, mobile phone, and even the Web. Finding the photo, you want is easy even if you've got a lot of digital elements on your computer. When importing, the software displays a thumbnail of the files so there isn't any confusion.

Design Features

Digital Scrapbook Artist is a great tool jam-packed with photo-realistic elements from backgrounds to fonts, frames to brushes, and all kinds of scrap embellishments. A few of the unique features to this digital scrapbooking program include the customizable brushes and the scissor and punch tools. There are twenty-four different types of scissor edges to choose from as well as a punch tool that functions like a real paper punch. The brushes allow you to add stitches, ribbon, and other stamp-like effects to your design. The text editor makes it easy to put text on a curved path. The software also has a pretty hefty photo editor that allows you to correct the color of images, fix red-eyes, add special effects, and enhance your images. Users can now take advantage of stencils and a blending tool. Editing photos has never been easier with the Photo Lab, which allows you to use over seventy effects and get rid of red-eyes, remove spots and blemishes, adjust color, and change the contrast, to name a few.

Output Options

Share your masterpieces in a multitude of ways from print to e-mail to exporting and uploading to the Internet. An interesting social component of Digital Scrapbook Artist is the online community the software works with through Daisy Trail. On this site, you upload your favorite digital scrapbook pages and the community of users can view and comment on them. It's also an ideal way to share your designs with friends and family. You can also export your projects into several different formats, including JPEG, PNG, BMP, and PDF.

Family Tree Poster

(Source: http://blogs.ancestry.com/ancestry/2009/03/04/creating-family-tree-posters-from-your-online-tree/)

Creating a family tree poster is a great way for your relatives to visualize how everyone is connected to one another. If possible, you should have a family tree poster displayed at every reunion so that new comers can be brought up to speed with regards to understanding their connection with everyone else in attendance. Your family tree poster will have the most impact when you go back as many generations as you can. There are several ways in which you can make a family tree poster. The quickest and easiest method that I have found is by using genealogy software—online or offline. We have already discussed in great detail the top three rated genealogy software—Family Tree Maker 2011, Family Tree Builder 4.0, and Legacy Family Tree 7.0. All three of these software packages have both online and offline features. The advantage of using the offline feature is the ability to design professional looking, custom family trees. The publishing service offered by genealogy software companies is a great feature that will make creating the family tree poster an easy and fun project after you have entered all of your family's information into the database.

One of the editors of Ancestry.com compiled an extensive, step-by-step guide to creating a family tree poster for those of you who are considering creating a family tree using the Family Tree Maker 2011 software, if you have a family tree on Ancestry.com. Keep in mind, Family Tree Maker 2011 and Ancestry.com linked online to MyCanvas publishing service. You can import your family tree from Family Tree Maker 2011or from Ancestry.com into MyCanvas that allows you to design and print your family tree for free, or order one in a variety of sizes. You can make a poster that includes as few as four generations or as many as nine. So, here are basic steps in creating your family tree poster on Ancestry.com, which is what I use.

Step 1: Build an Online Tree—or Upload an Existing Tree to Ancestry.com

If your family history information is stored on the desktop software program, Family Tree Maker 2011, you can export your tree as a GEDCOM file and then upload it to Ancestry.com. GEDCOM is the universal file sharing format for family history software.

When you create or upload your tree, you'll be asked to choose a privacy setting. No matter what setting you choose, information about people we believe to be living (based on the birth and death data you provide) is always hidden. Your name and contact information are hidden unless you choose otherwise.

Step 2: Create Your Family Tree Poster

You can now use the MyCanvas publishing service to create your family tree poster based on the information in your tree, and it is easy and fun. To access the MyCanvas publishing service, click the "Publish and Print" button from your online family tree. You can also click the "Print and Share" tab from the Ancestry.com home page, or just follow this link: http://mycanvas.ancestry.com.

From the vertical navigation menu at the top of the MyCanvas home page, click "Products" and then click "Family Tree Posters." Select your poster format and size. Family tree posters are available in a combination tree format, which has a bowtie shape, or a standard pedigree format. The size of your poster (20×16, 24×18, or 24×36) depends on the number of generations you want to include. You can make a combination tree poster with four, five, or seven generations or a standard tree poster with five, six, seven, eight, or nine generations.

If you have more than one online tree, choose the one you want to use and then pick a starting person for your poster. The starting person can be anyone in your tree. Name your project and then click the orange "Continue" button.

MyCanvas will automatically pull the relevant information from your tree to create your poster. If you have primary photos associated with the people in your tree, it will include those as well. If you have photos attached to a particular person but you haven't designated a primary photo, no photo will show up for that person (but you can easily add photos to your poster, as described below).

Step 3: Customize the Design of Your Poster

If you like the clean, simple look of your auto-generated poster, you can go ahead and click the "Order" button. But I'd recommend that you spend at least half an hour customizing your poster's look and feel. It's easy to do, and you'll be happier with the end result because it will reflect your own personality.

To change your poster's background just click the "Backgrounds" tab to explore the options. There are several tree backgrounds that are designed to be subtle enough that that they won't detract from your family history information. You can also use the advanced color palette to create a solid background in any color, or use the color picker to match a color in a photo.

If you want to add embellishments, click the "Other Content" tab to access thousands that you can drag and drop onto your poster. You then can move, resize, rotate, flip, copy, and combine embellishments to get the look you want. There's also a folder that contains more than two hundred flags from different states and countries. Flags are a great way to indicate your ancestors' countries of origin while adding a splash of color to your poster.

Any photos that you've attached to your online tree will appear under the "Ancestry Records" tab. You can also upload photos directly to MyCanvas or import them from Flickr, MyFamily, SmugMug, or Picasa. To add a photo to your poster, grab the thumbnail, and drag it onto the page. You can either drop the photo into an image box or just place it wherever you want. Once a photo is on the page, you can easily move, crop, resize, and rotate it, add a border or frame and even make the photo transparent.

You'll want to zoom in on a particular area of your poster before you try to edit the text. Go to the Zoom icon on the top toolbar. When you move the slider bar or click the plus sign, a little box will appear in the top left corner of the main workspace, right under the Zoom icon. That box is a map of your poster. The red square inside the box is the panning tray. It shows you which section of your poster you are currently seeing in the main workspace. To move to a different section, just move the panning tray.

Step 4: Print and Share Your Family Tree Poster

Before you order a printed copy of your poster, be sure to preview it carefully to make sure there are no mistakes. Use the Zoom tool for this function. MyCanvas does not offer framing, but the posters come in standard sizes.

You can share your poster electronically with your family to get feedback from them before you order your poster. When you share a MyCanvas project, you can invite the people you're sharing with to purchase their own printed copy.

Family History DVD Movie

(Source: http://www.dvd-family-portrait.com/Bruce-Pittman-Resume.html)

Turning your family's history into a DVD movie is a project that I would not recommend that you do on your own, unless you have a background in movie production. However, creating a DVD movie is great way to transform your family history archives and a great legacy for your family. A DVD movie can also serve as a unique gift or be used to raise funds for your family. There are some basic steps in preparing for your DVD, whether you hire a professional movie producer (all or in part) or embark on this project, solo.

Preproduction Preparation

During preproduction, there are two things that you want to accomplish. The first is to have on hand a comprehensive record of your family's history. Second, is to make a DVD family portrait that will be great viewing for everyone. In order make your DVD movie interesting, consider mixing the photographic and film record of your family's history with short clips of news, sports, movies, and TV that reflected the times in which your family grew up. Taking a multigenerational approach to include great-great-grandparents, grandparents, parents, and your generation, will add interest of your DVD.

Production Process

To begin your DVD project, you should meet with the producer with the goal of accomplishing two things. Initially, the producer should have an opportunity to review your family's archives to get a sense of your family's history. Then you should discuss your ideas on the events of the times you'd like to include, as well as the music for your DVD. From this point, both you and the producer can determine the story you want to tell. This simply translates into what you want to say and how you want to say it. Based on this discussion, your producer can give you a detailed report with all the cost of the project clearly stated.

Voice-Overs

Voice-overs are usually done near the completion of the "final cut." One suggestion is to designate a family member to provide the "voice" or you can hire a professional actor to provide an expert third person view of your family. The choice is yours. There usually is no extra fee for using an actor but first confirm this with your producer.

Postproduction

At the conclusion of your review of the "first cut" of your DVD project, all the elements should be in place for the final creation of your project including all selected photos, slides, video, DVD, 8-mm and 16-mm films (and anything else). Next, you should plan and schedule film interviews, additional photography, changes with voice-overs, and music selections. Ideally, postproduction is the best time to select a title. At this point, with all your information, approvals, and thoughts and ideas in hand, your producer will make the "final cut." This process can take up to three months.

Pricing

The all-inclusive pricing of your family history DVD movie should include the following: digital transfers of all photographs, slides, and documents for use in your DVD family portrait; a DVD copy of all photographs, slides, and documents; digital transfers of all 8-mm and 16-mm video and DVD materials; a DVD copy of all 8-mm and 16-mm video and DVD material "uncut"; all research, acquisition, and digital transfers of documentary, film, and TV clips; all research, acquisition, and digital transfers of music material; a CD copy of preliminary music selections; filmed interviews of your family (if desired); additional photography (if desired); voice-over recording (if desired); additional acquisition and digital transfer of sound effects; between three and four months' editing of all the above material; a DVD copy of the "first cut"; a DVD Master of your finished movie with customized cover and label; and a DVD copy of your finished movie with customized cover and label.

Just to give you an idea about DVD movie pricing, here are several estimates. For a thirty-minute DVD, the approximate cost is about $4,000. A forty-five-minute DVD costs approximately $6,500.

A sixty-minute DVD is in the costs about $9,000. The length of your project depends on the size of your archive, the amount of filmed interviews, additional photography, and documentary material.

The maximum length recommended is sixty minutes. This is more than adequate to tell your story in an entertaining fashion. To give some idea of what a sixty-minute DVD may contain is just over 500 photographs, sixteen minutes of home movies, and a liberal amount of documentary material.

À la carte pricing is as follows: filmed interview is about $500 per day of filming, additional photography $250 per day filming, and voice-overs at a cost of $250 per day recording.

Payment for the project generally requires 25 percent on signing of the project; 50 percent on delivery of the first edited "rough assembly" version; 25 percent on delivery of the finished DVD family portrait. and a copy. Additional copies are $25 each.

Creating a Private Family Web Site

Why Have a Family Web Site?

Whether your desire is to preserve your family's history, organize a family reunion, or stay connected with family year around, you need a Web site. A Web site is the most efficient way to accomplish all three of these goals. If you are the family historian as I am or just involved in compiling family trees, genealogy information, or have talked to older family members and gathered stories from the past, you need a centralized place to house and preserve this information. My concern was what would happen if there was a fire or some other disaster that would destroy all of the photos, oral histories, and other documents that I had collected over the years and stored on my computer's hard drive? These are things that could never be replaced. The very thought of losing these priceless items is what motivated me to create a Web site for our family.

Now there are some families who may choose Web site for the sole purpose of family reunion planning. There are hosting sites available just for this purpose. Instead of mailing or phoning each of your family members every time there's a reunion update, simply send your invitees e-mails directing them to your family reunion Web site. There they will read up on all the great reunion ideas that you have planned. Complete details and maps will be accessible at all times and from anywhere. Family members will have a central place where they'll find all the answers to their questions about where and when your events take place, and how to get there.

Improved family communications is another reason to consider for creating a family Web site. These days, with so many families living at a distance from one another, creating a Web site is a great way to stay connected and to strengthen ties. Communications are much easier with a Web site and will allow family to stay in the loop with what is going on, even from across the world. A Web site allows you to continually add and update information, and other family members can contribute as well in this process. Now that you understand the importance of creating a Web site, this next section guides through the steps of choosing the right Web site for your family.

Factors to Consider When Choosing a Web site

(Source: http://ezinearticles.com/?Create-a-Family-Website&id=4029094)

Determine Your Family's Goals and Needs

When deciding upon which Web site to choose, you should carefully consider your options based on the goals and needs of your family. Some Web sites have more of a focus on genealogy research and preservation of your family's history, while others focus on family reunion planning. There are a few free Web sites available, but they generally offer fewer features. If you decide on the Web site that best suits your family's needs or goal you're your family primary goal is genealogy research and preserve your family's history, then you should choose a Web site hosting provider that provides links to genealogy databases. The best option in this instance would be myfamily.com. However, if primary focus of your family is to organize a family reunion and to or stay connected with family year around, then selecting one of the other Web-hosting providers such as Myevent.com. Other Web sites such as MyGreatBigFamily.com, or Yourfamily.com offer a combination of features.

Determine the Features You Need

Second, determine what Web site features you need. If your goals of our Web site are for general communications and family reunion planning, then select a Web site that offers a family reunion organizer.

Consider the Cost

Cost is an important factor when choosing a Web site. Some Web hosting fees are less expensive than others. Then too, there are few free family Web sites that will be discussed later, but typically offer fewer features.

Evaluate the Privacy and Security Features

Today privacy and security is of utmost importance. This is also the case when deciding on a Web site for your family. Most Web sites leave the option up to your family's Web site administrator as to who will have access to the site. I personally recommend that you don't make your Web site public for obvious reasons. Your family will want the assurance that no one outside of family has access to their personal information. But you can allow as many family members as your desire to be able to post stories, discussions, news, upload pictures, or update the family tree. Just as a general caution, some of the free family Web sites may lack the security your family needs to protect from loss of valuable information. This may be one good reason to pay a fee for the site. You may be paying for the security and safety of the content. In sum, you should carefully review various Web sites before choosing one. It's best to make a chart comparing the sites before you decide. The right Web site is the one that matches your family's goal and needs, offers suitable features, is reasonably priced, and is secure and private. Once your Web site has been chosen you need to plan its content.

What to Put on Your Web site?

(Source: http://ezinearticles.com/?Create-a-Family-Website&id=4029094)

content that you decide to have on your Web site will be driven by your family's goals and needs. In general, you will want to include photos with captions, written content (family stories, history, narratives, and journals), audio and video recordings, other important documents (scanned copies of birth, marriage, and death certificates), the family tree, and reunion information and plans. So let's review some of the popular Web sites and the unique features they offer.

MyGreatBigFamily.com

(Source: http://www.mygreatbigfamily.com/features.php)

MyGreatBigFamily.com is a Web site that comes preconfigured with everything you need to connect online with your relatives around the world and preserve your family's history. This is a secure Web site with a private password and is free from commercial advertisements. This Web site is further protected in that it only allows your family members, and those you give permission to, access to your site. It has an optionally enabled security feature that lets the Web site administrator screen all content that is uploaded before it appears on the site.

Costs

The fees are affordable allowing the whole family to be connected online. The cost for the yearly hosting plan that includes up to 5,000 photos is $139.95 or $159.95 for unlimited photo storage. It should be noted that there is also a one-time setup activation fee of $100.

There are multiyear discounts available.

Features

MyGreatBigFamily.com is loaded with many great interactive features that let your family stay in touch with each other, including the feature selector, family member homepage, family member listing, family explorer, message boards, live chat, family reunion organizer, event calendar, family slideshow, photo gallery, polls, family recipe section, game room, multi-photo up loader, video up loader, family story section, what's new discussion board, family trivia, family reunion, news/blogs, online newsletter, music jukebox, family clubhouse, in memory of section, guestbook, online links, random rotating banner, event reminder, and more.

Feature Selector

The feature selector allows you to enable or disable any of the site features for a customized appearance. There is no limit set on the time you can turn features off and on. For example, if your family has not advanced to the level of publishing an online newsletter, you can disable this feature. Alternatively, popular features such as message boards, event calendar, and photo gallery are the ones that you will keep in enabled mode.

Family Members' Homepage

A feature that is unique to this Web site is that every family or family member can have their own personal homepage within the site that they can maintain themselves. The family member pages are initially created by the site administrator. Each family member then can then log into their own Web page to customize the look and maintain the content on their page.

Each individual or family homepage includes a news blog, personal photo albums, member links, personal facts, and favorite off-site links. A personal facts link is automatically created on the member page that links that person's homepage with their personal information in the family member's database.

Family Members Listing

The family member listing section provides a location for family member to exchange their contact information and document important genealogical facts about themselves or family members. Additionally, family members can add their biographies, photos, and other important historical facts. There are fifty predefined categories that you can select from and customize.

Family Explorer

Family Explorer is a collection of online tools that allows you to research your family history using the information contained in your site. You are able to graphically explore family member relationships in your online family tree and view family and family member history. Included also in Family Explorer is a search engine that lets you quickly find out about family members, facts, dates, places, and family member time lines just to name a few.

Live Chat

Family members can schedule live chat sessions right in your personal chat room. This is a cost saving feature compared to the money spent using cell phone minutes.

Family Reunion Organizer

The Family Reunion Organizer is another one of those unique features offered by MyGreatBigFamily.com. As you will discover, planning a family reunion can be a daunting task without the proper organizational tools. The Family Organizer is a tool that helps to keep the family informed of reunion plans, maintains a who's coming list, sends out mass e-mails, provide links to local hotels, and distributes directions to events. Contact mailing lists can either be exported or printed out. The Family Reunion organizer may be beneficial for those planning smaller reunions with fewer than fifty attendees but will not likely contain all of the tools necessary to plan a family reunion of a larger scale.

Family Slideshow

Family Slideshow organizes the photos you select into a gallery that displays them in random order. You then have the option of displaying your photos on your computer or television.

Polls

You can create custom polls to survey the opinions of your family members regarding certain topics. For example, the poll feature is a handy tool that can be used when trying to plan for the next family reunion. Information that can be solicited includes the date and location of the next family reunion, selection of the reunion theme, preferred reunion activities, or any information you believe is pertinent to your family reunion.

Family Recipes

The family recipe feature is probably one of those you will likely disable. If your family is like mine, no one really likes to share favorite recipes and their culinary secrets. But for those families where sharing is not a problem, consider this feature as a depository for creating a family cookbook in the future.

Game Room

Game Room is one of the new features of MyGreatBigFamily.com that allows your family members to play an assortment of fun games right within your Web site. There are a variety of fun games available for all ages.

Did You Know

Did You Known is an educational feature that randomly displays historical facts about family members on the homepage.

Family Stories

Recorded family stories such as those obtained from oral history interviews have a place on MyGreatBigFamily.com.

What's New

What's New keeps track of the most recent changes on your site which makes it easy for you and your family members to quickly find all the latest updates.

Family Trivia

You can create fun trivia games or contest to document interesting family facts and events. This is can be a springboard for activities at the family reunion.

Family Museum

Family museum is a photo gallery to archive memorabilia from your family past.

Schedulable Newsletter

Schedulable Newsletter was recently added as a new feature that allows you to create a newsletter on the Web site then automatically sends it out to family members on a scheduled day of the month. All that's needed is for you to choose a date each month for the newsletter to go out and the system does all the rest automatically.

Music Jukebox

This new feature, Music Jukebox, gives family members the option to personalize their homepage with licensed background music. Multiple genres of licensed music can be selected from an extensive library that can be played across all the pages within individual's personal homepage without interruption.

Family Clubhouse

You can create an unlimited number of special interest clubs for your family members. Ideas for special interest groups might include a history and genealogy group, book club, and cooking club. Each club created has its own home page, message board, and photo gallery. Site administrator can assign individual family members as club owners (moderator) to oversee and maintain the club pages.

In Memory of

In memory of is a special place on your family's Web site to pay tribute to family members who have passed on.

Guestbook

Guestbook is a place for Web site visitors to let your family know they have visited the site.

Offsite Links

Offsite links connect you and your family to other Web sites of interest.

Scrolling Marquee

Is a prominently displayed marquee that horizontally scrolls text across the main page of your Web site to welcome visitors or relay important facts or news to your family.

Random Rotating Banner

Random Rotating Banner allows you to add interesting visual effects such as random rotating picture strips of family members.

Myfamily.com

(Source: http://trees.ancestry.com/pt/learnmore/gedcom.aspx and http://www.myfamily.com/isapi.dll?c=home&htx=Activities)

General Information

Myfamily.com is a password-protected Web site that you set up. Only you and those family members that you invite to join can access the Web site. You can set up your own personal online community for your family, inviting as many family members as you desire. With myfamily.com, your family can keep everyone updated by posting pictures, news items, calendar events, video clips, audio files, blog entries, bios, etc. Everyone can interact using the discussions message board. What makes this Web site unique is that it's the only site that caters to the family historian with a family history message center and the capability to upload family trees.

Web site Features

Myfamily.com offers a unique service to help families and other close-knit groups stay connected. Here are some of the many things you can do with your own private family site. With this Web site, I am able to preserve my family's heritage with the many wonderful features they offer. Myfamily.com has partnered with Ancestry.com to administer the family tree section of the Web site. Ancestry.com has the world's largest online resource of family history documents and family trees.

Cost

Myfamily.com there are two basic fees, one for the Web site hosting and the other for genealogy research. There is a small yearly membership fee of $9.95 for the first year and $29.95 for each year, thereafter. This is inexpensive compared to what you would normally pay to keep in touch with family members via phone bills and/or mailings. The site allows for 100 MB of storage and you can purchase an additional MB if needed.

Ancestry.com which provides administrative support for the family trees created in myfamily.com has made available a variety of genealogy records to develop your family's tree. With the two types of paid memberships made available through Ancestry.com, you will have access to all the tools needed to develop your family's tree. If you would like to restrict your research to just the United States., then the monthly fee after the initial free fourteen-day trial period is $19.95 per month or $155.40 annually for the U.S. Deluxe Membership. Also, there is the World Deluxe Membership that carries a monthly fee of $24.99 and annual fee of $299.40. Both the U.S. and World Deluxe memberships allow access to U.S. census, birth, marriage, death, immigration, military records, and more. Find just one name match and you could add entire branches to your tree instantly.

Ask questions. Offer advice. Collaborate and share with other Ancestry members. However, features not offered in the U.S.

Deluxe Membership includes a link to World Collections. You are able to explore historical records from the United Kingdom, Ireland, and other locations around the globe. There is unlimited access to everything on Ancestry.com. Discover new records and images as they are added every week!

Customized Homepage

It's easy to personalize the look of the Web site at any time with one click. Select from a variety of professionally designed looks or easily create your own. You are able change the theme, background image, and color combinations. Themes can be changed as often as you like. Themed backgrounds reflect seasons, holidays, and other special events such as birthdays and sports just to mention a few. Additionally, family members can have their own personal Web page within the site that they can maintain themselves. The main family homepage is initially created by the site administrator. Each family member then can then log into their own Web page to customize the look and maintain the content on their page. Each individual Web page includes a profile photo, biography, blog, e-mail inbox, and a section that allows you to post notes, personal profile photo, links, personal facts, and favorite off-site links.

News

News lets members keep up on family news, easily share news items with all site members, reply to previous messages (threaded), and annotate items with multimedia content. Members can optionally receive notification via e-mail when news items are posted.

Calendar

The calendar keeps you up-to-date with family events. Birthdays and anniversaries can be automatically added to the calendar. Plan reunions, parties, and other family or group get-togethers and receive e-mail reminders so you won't forget anything important.

Photos

Photo allows members to store and share photos with site members. Members may annotate and organize album content.

File Cabinet

Your family can upload any computer file to this area to share with other site members (such as legal documents, family records, shareware applications, and so on). I have used this feature to upload scanned files in Microsoft Word containing obituaries, birth certificates, death certificates, or any family history documents your desire to preserve.

Reviews

Your family can share opinions with other site members about movies, music, Web sites, and other experiences in the reviews section.

Chat/Who's Online

This feature shows which family members are currently online and lets members instantly communicate with them. Members may also enter their site chat area and hold a private group discussion.

Family Communication

Online communications with myfamily.com has never been easier. Through its inbox, you can send e-mail to all site members without requiring them to enter each member's e-mail address.

What I love about this portal is that a photo of both sender and receiver is attached to each email adding personal touch.

Myfamily.com is a great social networking site. Users are able to generate 'Family Groups' so that they can better manage who they display information and send photos to or contact as part of a group message. You may want to split family members into groups on the basis of what family branch they are linked, geographical location, or surname.

Family Trees

The Family Tree section of myfamily.com graphically allows you to share your genealogy by uploading a family tree file (GEDCOM file). Your family members don't need a separate software application to view and browse the tree, it's done for you online. This feature will be most useful to the family's historian. Through Ancestry.com, you can upload an existing tree file from a family tree software program; you are already using or build a new one. The family tree software data files that Ancestry.com directly supports are Family Tree Maker (. ftw), Family Tree Maker backup files (. fbk), Personal Ancestral File (. paf), Family DataBase (. fdb), Legacy 3.0 (. leg), Zipped gedcom and images (. gedz). The uploading process itself is quite easy. You just simply locate and select the appropriate family tree file on your hard drive, upload it to Ancestry.com, and Ancestry will interpret the file correctly and create your tree. On the other hand, you can create a GEDCOM file from your family tree software and upload it to Ancestry.com. GEDCOM compatible files are those with a common file format that allows different family tree software programs to communicate with each other. Nearly all family tree software supports importing family trees from a GEDCOM file as well as exporting to GEDCOM format.

Family Tree Uploading

The uploading file feature of Ancestry.com by way of myfamily.com was most beneficial to me. It was quite a few years after entering my family's information originally created in Family Tree Maker that I was now able to upload the family tree to the family tree section of our family's Web site on myfamily.com. This was wonderful discovery for me knowing that I did not have to import the information of hundreds relatives all over again. This feature saved me countless hours of work. Myfamily.com features also allow you to build your family tree.

Tree Building Tools

Both the U.S. Deluxe and World allows you to search just one name with the chance of adding an entire branch to your tree instantly. You can ask questions, offer advice, and collaborate with other Ancestry members with regards to posted family trees. With a paid subscription to Ancestry.com, you have access to U.S. census, birth, marriage, social security death index, immigration, military records, and more.

Newly added features in the family tree includes the ability to associate pictures and scanned documents to source citations you have created in your family tree. Sources are birth certificates, death certificates, marriage certificates, headstones, obituaries, immigration and emigration records, and much more.

Recipes

Preserve traditional family recipes from fading away or getting lost. Share your most popular family favorites with others who enjoy good food.

Family History

Publish and archive those treasured stories of your family. Let others read your account and then respond with their own version of favorite family anecdotes, telltales, and personal memories.

Multimedia Supported

In myfamily.com, not only are you able to upload family trees, you can also upload and catalog your ancestral photos. Additionally, myfamily.com is multimedia supported, allowing g you to add oral history videos, audio recording as well as written family stories. In the previous section of this book, the process for conducting an oral history was discussed. In myfamily.com Web site, you have a secure place to preserve your family's history in one location.

Yourfamily.com

(Source: http://www.yourfamilywebsite.com)

Just like the other two Web sites, Yourfamily.com is a password-protected site, so only your family and friends who have the password can view your family Web site. Your family Web site will allow you to add unlimited photos and we take care of creating the high-quality thumbnails.

You can add .JPG photos up to 200K in size to the Web site. Basic features of this Web sites includes a family blog, message board, photo album, guest book, favorite Web sites, and list of events. The advantage of this Web site is that it is free. However, many of the features offered by the other two Web sites are not available on this Web site.

FamilyLobby.com

Familylobby.com is another free Web site that you can update to additional paid features.

Family Pages are personalized Web sites designed to help families stay in touch, celebrate birthdays, share photos, and explore and preserve their family history. All it takes is for one family member to create Family Pages on MyHeritage.com, and invite other members of the family to join. All members are allowed and encouraged to contribute. It's a great way to bring families together!

MyHeritage.com

(Source: http://www.myheritage.com)

MyHeritage.com is a free, private, and secure family Web site loaded with many great features. It's private in that only members that you invite can access it. You have the option to choose to make your family's Web site public for the whole world to visit or private where only family members have access.

Family Tree Building

Treasure your family heritage and present it online! Showcase your family tree on your site with attractive visual reports. If you're a professional genealogist, you can upload your GEDCOM file; if you're a family history beginner, you can download a free Family Tree Builder and use it to put together your family tree and publish it online on your family site in one click. Every family member visiting your site will see a personalized version of the family tree tailored for him or her, showing them visually how they are related to any other person appearing in the family tree or in any of the family photos.

Download Family Tree Builder, our free genealogy software for putting together your family tree. It's not only completely free of ads and spyware, but it's also one of the best genealogy software programs you'll find. It has original, easy-to-use pages that let you grow your family tree visually. It runs in thirty-four languages and lets you create and print your family tree in several languages. Bring your family tree to life with photos and documents and use our ground-breaking face recognition technology to annotate your photos and discover the identity of people you don't recognize in your old family photos. With a few mouse clicks, you can publish your family tree to the Internet, on your own family Web site and share it with others.

Genealogy Research

MyHeritage.com's Research is a search engine built specifically for genealogy, capable of searching hundreds of major genealogy databases in a single query. It's the most comprehensive genealogy research tool existent today and the first of its kind. In simple terms, this search engine runs each query simultaneously in hundreds of genealogy databases, aggregates the results, and displays them in one consolidated report. This gives you more genealogy search power than has ever been available before, in a simple, friendly, and convenient interface.

So if you want to learn more about your heritage, or find information about your ancestors, you've come to the right place. Search over 1526 genealogy databases with one "super" search, or focus on a smaller subset of databases that interest you. Research several variants of a last name with one search to maximize hits and explore new avenues for research based on alternative spellings of a name. You can search multiple databases for multiple spelling variations, at once. Getting started is easy. Go to the New Search page, then type in the name of an ancestor, even just a last name, and click Search and that's it! MyHeritage.com Research does the rest, combing the Internet for relevant information in an unparalleled collection of the world's best genealogy resources—around 1526 of them to date. It queries Web sites, databases, archives, and message boards; covering all genealogy records including census records, family trees, immigration records, military records, medical records, cemetery records, court, land and probate documents, and other informational sources, such as newspapers, telephone directories, and more.

Their high-quality collection of resources is maintained by the dedicated team of genealogists at MyHeritage.com in order to provide you with the best chances of finding your ancestors.

What's more, the MyHeritage team is constantly scouring the Internet for new genealogy databases and updating MyHeritage.com Research to benefit from valuable new sources of information as they emerge, so you will always have the best information at your fingertips. That's why MyHeritage.com Research gives you more relevant results than any other genealogy resource or search engine.

Message Boards

The genealogy message boards are for sharing useful family history information with other users. You can search for a particular name or subject, or simply browse through the message boards below. Once you find an appropriate message board, visit it and click "Post new topic" to post a new message, or reply to any of the messages on it.

Photos and Video Sharing

This groundbreaking face recognition technology lets you organize your photos automatically and tie your photos to individuals in your family tree. Afterwards, you can automatically find more photos of your family members or your ancestors that other users have uploaded. You can finally discover the identity of unknown people in old family photos. You can even find other people around the globe who look exactly like you. MyHeritage.com is great for historic family photos. All photos are searchable, and even comments made by other users on photos can be searched. If a photo has a dedication on its reverse side, you can insert it too. If a photo is in poor condition, use our professional photo restoration services to bring it back to prime. There is no other Web site on the Internet that can match the sophisticated online photo handling on MyHeritage.com.

Organize Family Events

On your family site, you get a full-featured online calendar which can automatically read all important family events from your family tree (if you've got one) so you won't have to enter any birthday or anniversary yourself—and you and your family members will never miss an important family event again. It's probably the most beautiful calendar you've seen to date and there are even pictures of family members next to each event.

Family Applications

MyHeritage.com offers Family News so you and your family members can keep abreast of all that is happening in the family. Private message boards are great for holding family discussions. There is a Recipes application for sharing and treasuring the family's unique dishes. Then there is the Poll Application for gathering quick opinions on any topic. The Member Address Book is a nice feature and can be used to keep current updates on the whereabouts of a family member.

MyHeritage.com now has a new application, Advanced Medical History, for sharing medical information securely within the family and keeping track of genetic disorders.

Community Chat Room

With Community Chat Room, you can keep in touch not just with your family members on your own site, but explore the MyHeritage.com community and find other members who share your interests. Visit other Web sites, explore, and search through millions of photos uploaded by other users and run searches across all public family trees uploaded to MyHeritage.com.

Upgrading

MyHeritage.com allows you to create as many Web sites as you like. Each site has a subscription plan. Basic plans are free but if you want more storage, more members, larger family trees, and more features, go premium with the Premium or Premium Plus plans. Only one family member needs to subscribe the site, all other site members enjoy the site for free.

Chapter 6

Family Reunion Planning

Family Reunion Defined

The family reunion is an event or a function in which family members gather at a certain venue and share their experiences. Family reunions may comprise of events such as picnics, city tours, games, dinners, and other fun activities. Family reunions help in staying in touch with the extended family members. Family reunions can also be used as a social networking platform for making new connections and strengthening the older ones. These new connections will not only help you emotionally, but also can help you professionally as well (Source: http://www.livestrong.com/article/78716-purpose-family-union).

Family Reunion Statistics

When reviewing research regarding reunion statistics, I was surprised to learn of the number of Americans estimated to attend family reunions yearly. Edith Wagner, editor of U S based Reunions Magazine, in an interview cited by The Vancouver Sun on August 25, 2007, she shared that about 200,000 families across North America get together for reunions each year. Reunions Magazine regularly tracks reunion trends and statistics through their ongoing surveys. She added that most reunions have about fifty attendees, and they usually take place on a weekend (Source: http://www.canada.com/vancouversun/story.html?id=ce544728-3f85-4e31-8bec-9c7ed4537d42&p=1). According to familyreunion.com, an estimated 20 million people go to 400,000 family reunions each year. Each event averages seventy-nine attendees (Source: http://www.familyreunion.com/?serv=adcenter.dbf). So, what is it about family reunions that people are motivated to attend them year after year? Let's look at some reason why families have reunions.

Why Have a Reunion?

As Laura Ramirez puts it, "Family is essential because we all yearn to feel like we belong to something greater than ourselves." This quote represents the main reason why families have reunions. While family connectedness is crucial, other reasons for having family reunions vary across the board. A study conducted by Reunions Magazine in conjunction with the Department of Hotel, Restaurant and Tourism Management, East Stroudsburg University of Pennsylvania discovered that 57 percent of all reunions were organized to help keep members in touch, while over 28 percent wanted children to learn about their family heritage. Other reasons included to get everyone together before a family elder died, to mark a special birthday, anniversary, or holiday. Some individuals didn't even remember or know how their reunions got started but could recall attending them as children (Source: http://www.reunionsmag.com/advertise/opportunities_research2.html).

Your reunion is not at all unusual if it starts out of a suggestion made by a family member at a funeral. Many times when family members who haven't seen each other for some time meet at funeral they begin to reminiscence about the happier times of life. During this time of reminiscing, family members recognize the need to start meeting, to celebrate life under happier circumstances. Oddly enough, family reunions are quite similar to funerals except for one important fact; funerals are events that focus on the celebration or remembrance of just one person. Reunions celebrate the whole family. If a reunion is a new idea for your family, some members may not be ready. If so, you should not give up on your quest to organize a family reunion. When dealing with resistant family members you have two options. One option is to delay the idea of organizing your reunion for another time. Second, you can continue with willing members. Reluctant members may join a future reunion. The latter is my preference for reasons that I will share with you.

I can remember when my brother Elijah and I began the process of organizing our family's reunion; we did meet resistance from several family members. The resistance came when we wanted to extend invitations to family members of other branches of our family tree and to those who lived in other states. I believe this resistance came out of fear. Fear of not being accepted by other family members. Fear of not having enough financial resources to host a large reunion. Fear of not having enough manpower to plan a reunion that everyone will enjoy. In my opinion, these are the top three reasons why you will meet resistance when it comes to organizing your reunion. Because my brother and I were persistent and organized in our efforts, the resistant family members eventually joined rank. Thus far, we have a clear definition of what a family reunion is and understand the reasons given why families have reunions. Additionally, we have uncovered some of the obstacles faced when organizing a reunion. Now let's explore why it is important for families to have reunions.

Why Is It Important to Have Reunions?

I believe that it is essential for families to have reunions. I find that some family members often have a nonchalant attitude when it comes to participating in their reunions. These are the very same individuals who live of life of isolation and disconnectedness. I know that in my own family, it took many years to convince certain individuals to participate in our reunions. Once they did participate, the family reunion became more of a celebration to look forward to as they began to see the many benefits of getting together. There are a number of very important reasons for families to have reunions; some reasons have been previously mentioned, but we will explore them in detail now. There were two articles in USA Today's travel section that listed the importance of family reunions that we will examine. (Source: http://traveltips.usatoday.com/importance-family-reunions-52377.html and http://traveltips.usatoday.com/purpose-family-reunion-52387.html).

Rekindling Relationships

With our busy lives today, it is very easy to lose touch with family members, especially those who live in other states. Family reunions can help you reconnect with long-lost cousins, aunts, uncles, or anyone whom you have not kept in touch with over the years. You may even discover family members you didn't even know you had, while attending your reunion. Bonds are often strengthened during reunions.

Learn of Your Heritage

Family reunions provide for the opportunity to perpetuate the memory your ancestors through diligent study and research into your family's past. According to genealogy.com, about 28 percent of reunions are put together for younger family members to learn about their heritage. This occurs when elder family members share stories about the start of the family tree at the reunion. Depending on a family's own unique heritage, you may hear stories about slavery, war, famine, and immigration. Knowing your family history is very important for each member of the family because it tells them about their background and helps them in understanding their heritage (Source: http://www.livestrong.com/article/78716-purpose-family-union).

Promote Unity and Bonding

There are many ways in which family reunions promote a sense of unity and strengthen family bonds. You will find that most reunion activities are centered on these two themes that begin upon the arrival at the particular venue (hotel, resort, etc.). First off, everyone stays at the same venue and registers under the same family name. During registration, all family reunion participants will receive a name tag in the family's name to wear each day of the reunion. The wearing of reunion tee shirts fosters unity in that everyone wearing them will be recognized as part of the same family clan. The one thing that I enjoy at family reunion functions as the family historian is the sharing of the family's history and displaying the family tree. These two activities, I believe, are the most instrumental in fostering a sense of connectedness. The family tree is a visual representation of the relationships between family members of several generations. When individuals can visualize how they are genetically connected to one another, this promotes unity and bonding.

Role Modeling

Role modeling is often something that you don't hear about as being an important part of family reunions. I think this is because many times elder family members aren't always cognizant of the fact that they are setting an example for the younger generations. It's been often said that children learn by watching or by example. This can be said true of younger adults as well. For example, I had shared previously that there was great emphasis placed on getting a college education and to achieve the highest level of education possible in my family. I am proud when I attend my family reunion to see that I have elder family members who are physicians and lawyers; those who hold master's degrees and PhDs.

Scientific findings confirm role modeling as a strong predictor of behavior. Social psychologists developed the idea that people role model each other. In other words, they do what they see other people doing. If we think about the many ways that we do things that other people do, we can agree that role modeling has shaped our behaviors. For example, how many times have we purchased clothing based on Hollywood trends? College students have often started drinking alcohol because everyone else a party was drinking and they did not want to feel left out. Most young people follow the crowd. However, elder people are immune to doing things a certain way because that is what others do as well.

Alfred Bandura, an American psychologist and a social behavioralist, is mostly remembered for his Social Learning Theory. He worked with Richard Walters in research on social learning and aggression in children. This research work led to the crucial role in modeling behavior simply by observation. His famous experiment is included in every first year psychology test book and is known as the Bobo doll experiment. The Bobo doll experiment was tested out in 1961 to lend credence to his beliefs that human behavior is fashioned by learned behaviors though imitation and copying, otherwise known as modeling. He did not believe our genes determined behavior. The results proved that children who were exposed to an aggressive adult handling the Bobo doll, became aggressive themselves once the adult left the room and they were alone to play with the doll. This study, as well as a host of others studies that followed, gives credence to the belief that all human behavior is learned, through social imitation and copying, rather than inherited through genetic factors. Thus, when we come together for family reunions, we should be mindful of example we are setting for the younger generations (Source: http://factoidz.com/role-modeling-children-are-taught-by-example and http://www.experiment-resources.com/bobo-doll-experiment.html#ixzz1OKmIdz9W).

Keeps Family Tree Updated

You may find that, as is the case with our family, during the family reunion is usually the only time that you can find to update the family tree. In the past, our family utilized forms in similar format of the family group sheets to update each family's information. However, over the years, we have found this process to be redundant especially to those family members who are beyond childbearing years. We have a new process that we are trying to implement, which involves having family members to update their family's tree on our Web site. Unfortunately, not everyone has computers; especially the older generation, therefore, updating information at the reunion is the best method for these individuals.

Have Fun

Last, but certainly not the least, important reason we gather together for our family reunions is to have fun and enjoy each other's company. While family reunion planning can be a daunting task, you must incorporate fun activities of all age groups in order to keep people coming back for reunion after reunion. Many of activities will be explored later in this book, which brings us to the next section of the book, steps in organizing your family reunion.

Steps in Organizing Your Reunion

Good organizational skills go a long way when planning a family reunion. Actually, it can make or break your reunion. Reunions should be organized in such a way that each and every family member attending should find something that he or she can enjoy. The basic steps in planning a successful reunion involve establishing a reunion planning committee, forming necessary subcommittees, conducting a prereunion survey, selecting a date, choosing a location, setting a budget, planning activities, and sending out invitations.

Planning family reunions these days is easier with the available software on the market to help in your organizing efforts. Family Reunion Organizer by RootsMagic, Reunion Planner Standard and Professional Edition, and Reunite by Minutiea Software are probably the most popular softwares. Their features are very similar, with each offering an address book that organizes individual and family information. Other basic reunion information that can be entered includes the reunion theme, location, date, and logo. Additionally, you can create a schedule of meals and activities. Items such invitations, name tags, mailing lists and labels, budget and expense worksheets, just to mention a few, can be printed out on your computer. Prices of various software packages range from about $30 to $160.

Those of you who would desire a quick and easy reunion organizer/planner you can refer to appendix A. Here you will find a simple twenty-four-month family reunion time line planner. This reunion time line planner was adapted from the reunion timetable found in 11th Edition of Reunions Workbook (Source: 11th Edition of Reunions Workbook by Reunions Magazine and http:/familyreunionhelper.com/reunion_checklist.php).

The Reunion Planning Committee

Now that you have the tools necessary to plan your reunion, next on your list is to set up a reunion planning committee. This is one of the most important processes in planning your reunion. The individuals chosen or who volunteer to serve should be those family members that are team players and who will be committed to see projects through to completion. Also, it's best to match individuals to positions that best fit their personality, interests, or expertise. If you know that Aunt Bessie loves to cook, then she should be considered to serve on the food committee. On the other hand, you should not consider a family member who is basically an introvert to serve on the activities committee. This person might be better suited for the history and research committee.

After laying the foundation for committee member selection, the rest should be simple. At this point a meeting should be organized with as many relatives as possible to get everyone's input. The best way I have found to get everyone together for the initial meeting is to plan it during a holiday dinner or family picnic. Anyone can start the conversation about the plans for family reunion. Afterward, family should vote for whom they think will be best qualified for various positions.

I believe that it is important for everyone who desires to serve on the reunion planning committee to fully understand their responsibilities before making this commitment.

I often find that individuals take on positions that they lack full knowledge of and may overestimate their qualifications and underestimate their time commitment for these positions.

What has been explained for you here is a description of each position within the reunion planning committee.

Chairperson or President

As with any organization, a leader is necessary. The same applies when planning a family reunion. The chairperson or president can be an elected officer or volunteer. This person should be someone who has good people and communication skills. This is a vital characteristic, since throughout the reunion planning process you will need someone who is able to motivate people to complete their assigned tasks. An excellent point that Mr. Spiffy makes is that the chairperson should be someone that everyone respects and will listen to (Source: http://family-reunion.com/organize.htm). The chairperson will be responsible for scheduling and presiding over all reunion planning committee meetings. This also includes notifying all committee members of meetings. The committee chairperson will be additionally responsible for overseeing all reunion activities. The chairperson can delegate responsibilities to the other members as often as deemed necessary.

Co-chairperson or Vice-President

One of the best pieces of advice that I can give to all reunion planners is to always have a backup for every position. So is true for the position of reunion chairperson or president. We all know that life is unpredictable and things happen. It would be a shame for one person to be solely responsible for a particular task or tasks and something happened to that person and the reunion plans are thwarted. To prevent this from happening, I strongly recommend selecting a reunion co-chairperson/vice president. This position can also be filled by one who is elected or volunteers. The co-chairperson/vice president will assist and support the chairperson/president in his or her duties during the designated tenure. Additionally, the co-chairperson/vice president will perform the duties of the chairperson/president in his or her absence or inability to act. The co-chairperson/vice president will be responsible for attending all reunion planning meetings.

Secretary

The secretary can be an elected officer or volunteer. The responsibilities of the secretary include recording all meeting minutes as well as reading the preceding meeting minutes. All financial transactions including account credits and disbursement will be recorded by the secretary. Additionally, the secretary has the authority to designate an assistant to assist with the approval of the planning committee. The treasurer, along with the secretary will assure that all financial records and statements are accurate and disbursements and receipts are balanced.

Treasurer

The treasurer, in my estimation, is probably the second most important position of the reunion planning committee. With this in mind, the treasurer must be someone that can be trusted and is a good financial manager. The treasurer will be responsible for the receipt and disbursements of all monies. The treasurer will assure that all financial transactions are recorded and that the preceding meeting transactions are read at all meetings. The treasurer has the authority to designate an assistant that will assist the treasurer in performing his or her duties. Mr. Spiffy recommends as a safety feature that the treasurer sets up a checking account that requires two signatures on checks (Source: http://family-reunion.com/subcomm.htm).

As far as the tenure of these key positions, this should be determined by the planning committee. Our family's reunion planning committee has kept the same people in their positions year after year. However, if an individual no longer decides to hold a particular position then we vote on a replacement. This process has been successful for our family over the past seventeen years.

When taking your reunion to the next level, you will need to establish reunion planning committees in each state or region your family chooses to have a reunion, granted there are enough family members for this committee. If not, then designated volunteers from other states can lend their help to other families in other states.

The next step in the process, now that you have your core reunion planning committee organized, should be to schedule a formal meeting to work out the specific details of the reunion and determine what subcommittees will be needed.

Reunion Planning Meetings

Regular meetings help to keep family members accountable for assigned duties. It is also the best way to track reunion planning progress. Generally, meetings should be held monthly. However, four to six weeks prior to the reunion, you should meet weekly. The format for your family's meeting minutes can be found in appendix A. It's a good idea to collect dues at each meeting to help defray cost of unexpected expenses. Whatever amount you are interested in collecting should be between $2 and $5, not to create an undue burden on family members.

Pre-reunion Survey

Pre-reunion surveys are a must when planning a reunion. It's the best way that I know of, to guide your reunion planning efforts.

Otherwise you will be planning in the dark. This is not to say that you will be able to plan activities to appease everyone. However, at least you will have a good idea of what activities the majority of your family members have an interest in participating.

The pre-reunion survey should be distributed to family members soon after you have had your first reunion planning committee meeting and before you set the final date for your reunion. I recommend sending out the pre-reunion survey eighteen to twenty-four months prior to your reunion. In appendix A, there is a sample pre-reunion survey that our family used. As you see later, the Communications Committee bears the responsibility for distributing the pre-reunion. The quickest and most efficient way for this to be done is by e-mail. Sending anything by mail these days is obsolete and costly.

Reunion Subcommittees

After you have compiled the results of your pre-reunion survey, you will have a better idea of the size of your reunion and the subcommittees needed. Mr. Spiffy's Web site provides a comprehensive listing of the various reunion planning subcommittees that you may or may not need, depending on the size of your reunion (Source: http://family-reunion.com/subcomm.htm). As a general rule of thumb, the larger the reunion, the more committees you will need. With the information provided on Mr. Spiffy's and from my own personal experience planning family reunions, I will review the responsibilities of each subcommittee.

Finance Committee

The finance committee is responsible for developing a budget for all reunion activities and works in conjunction with the treasurer and secretary in their duties. This committee determines all reunion costs, itemizes all reunion expenses, sets up a bookkeeping system, and assists in fundraising efforts. The finance committee is also responsible for setting up a bank account in the name of the family reunion. Additionally, the finance committee records all cash receipts, disbursements that also include paying for all reunion expenses. This is a shared responsibility with the secretary and treasurer. Finally, the finance committee approves all budgetary requests submitted by other committees. The treasurer is a member of the finance committee and reports back to the reunion planning committee.

Food Committee

The food committee has the responsibility of planning and coordinating all reunion functions that involve food. Specifically, this involves selecting venues for hosting reunion events such as picnic facilities, banquets halls, cruise ships, and any equipment rental associated with the event. This committee plans and selects the menus, caterers or food preparers, and decorations. If food and other items require pick up or drop-off, the committee will make these arrangements. Finally, the committee is required to submit all contracts and budgets to the finance and reunion planning committee for final approval.

Activities Planning Committee

The activities planning committee plans and coordinates all activities associated with the reunion. This includes determining the type, length, location, and all entertainment associated with the reunion. The activities planning committee is perfect for younger family members and is a great way for them to get involved in the reunion planning efforts.

Communications Committee

(Source: http://www.temple.edu/fri/familyreunion/organize/communications.html)

This committee is responsible for compiling and updating the family directory. All reunion invitations and follow-up reminders will be forwarded by the communications committee. If you decide to send a survey to determine the specific details of your reunion, then this task can be carried out as well by the communications committee.

Communication with family members helps to generate information and maintain interest over the months of planning for the reunion. A computer makes it easier to handle all of your communications.

Compile the names, addresses, and telephone numbers of as many family members as you can find through your family network. Note how each person is related to the family.

The first communication may just be a notice that a family reunion is being planned. When the date, location, and facility have been confirmed, a second notice should be send that includes all reunion costs. The second letter should go out at least four to six months before the reunion. If the location or facility has some particularly attractive features, include this information in the letter to keep family members interested. Be sure to set a definite date for registration and payment. It is necessary to know who will be coming to the reunion so that arrangements regarding food, trips and tours, and lodging may be finalized. A third and final follow-up letter should be sent closer to the due date. When you send out notifications regarding the registration fee, it's a good idea to offer several payment options. This would include payments by cash, money orders, or installments. Don't forget to include directions on how to get to the event using various modes of transportation. Some facilities may provide maps. Appendix A has several letters composed by various individuals in our family that you may find useful for your reunion.

Fundraising Committee

The fundraising committee is in charge of coordinating and carrying out all fundraising activities for the reunion. Fundraising functions can include skating parties, flee market sales, bus excursions, or any other creative ideas your family can come up with to raise money legally. The fundraising committee works very closely with the finance committee.

History and Research Committee

The history and research committee is responsible for the collection, compilation, and updating of the family history. This includes identifying and communicating with unknown family members. Other responsibilities that may be assigned are creating, maintaining, and distributing the family directory, that is, if you don't have a communication committee. Members of this committee are responsible for notifying the family's historian and genealogical researcher of all family births, marriages, and deaths. The members of this committee should be selected from every branch of the family tree or region to facilitate data collection and communication. The family's historian and genealogical researcher must be a member of this committee.

Photography/Video Committee

Preserving your family's memories is vital. In the years to come, future generations can refer back to the photos captured as evidence of your family's unity. Many times families have someone already in their family who is a professional photographer. If not, one should be hired. The photography committee is responsible for making sure that all aspects of the reunion carefully captured. If a video is to be made of the reunion, this committee also has the responsibility for lining up a camcorder or hiring someone to create the video tape.

After the reunion, the photography committee should make copies of the photos or video available to family members, and decide on a price that will cover the cost. This can also be utilized as a fundraising event.

Hotel/Accommodations Committee

The hotel and accommodations committee is responsible for selecting accommodations for visiting guests, such as hotels or resorts. This includes, but is not limited to, contract negotiations and approval. Usually, blocks of rooms are reserved and negotiated at group-discount rate. When reserving over twenty rooms, a free hospitality suite can be negotiated and used to house one family (usually the chairperson/president and his family). The hospitality suite can also be used as the room for family registration or both. Once negotiations are complete, all contracts are submitted to the finance committee for final approval.

Welcoming Committee

(Source: http://www.familydetails.com/community/Family-Reunion-Guide/Greeting-Them-With-a-Smile.aspx)

The welcoming committee is responsible for greeting all guests at the check-in/registration table as they arrive to and throughout the reunion. They are the ones distributing reunion materials such as goodie bags, souvenir booklets, name tags, etc. If you have a put together some formal events that will be occurring at specific times, you can also distribute programs to your family members as they arrive so they can have a better idea of what to expect. Be sure to include information where nearby restaurants, nightclubs, malls, can be found in case they may want to venture out on their own during down time.

Try to get four or five individuals to be a part of your welcoming committee. Ideally, the welcoming committee should be composed of individuals representing different branches of the family tree there with you. This is so that everyone registering will have a familiar face checking them in and welcoming them to the reunion. Those that volunteer for or are selected to serve on this committee should be family members who have bubbly personalities. We all know who they are in our families. They are the ones who we label as "perky" or "smiley." Nothing is worse than being greeted by a grumpy, miserable person. This can be a real turn off.

Transportation Committee

(Source: How to Plan Memorable Family Reunions | eHow.com http://www.ehow.com/how_5088847_plan-memorable-family-reunions.html#ixzz1D9Vkqk3N)

The transportation committee coordinates the pickup and drop-off of guests. This may involve the rental of van or bus transportation. If a vehicle rental is necessary, the committee representative will submit a budget to the finance committee for final approval. Additionally, this committee is responsible for providing directions to various reunion events.

One of the most important tasks in family reunion planning is logistics. Within the transportation committee you will need someone to provide directions, pick up people from the airport, and to give rides when necessary. Whoever assumes this responsibility must be an individual who is organized, can keep track of multiple schedules, and provide rides or rental car information to anyone coming from out of town. Make this person the point person for any logistical information about the reunion.

Set Up and Cleanup Committee

The set up and cleanup committee is in charge of setting up and taking down chairs, tables, and other items for the reunion. This committee is also responsible for setting and taking down of all reunion decorations. The committee doesn't have to do all the work themselves but can solicit help from other willing family members.

Let's take a look back where we are in the reunion planning process. Thus far, we have established our core committee, the reunion planning committee. Within the reunion planning committee, we have a chairperson/president, cochairperson/vice president, secretary, and treasurer, all fully aware of their responsibilities. From this committee and based on the results of your pre-reunion survey, subcommittees are formed. After several reunions planning committee meetings, other important reunion decisions will be made such as the reunion date, location, lodging venue, theme, budget, and activities.

Time Needed to Plan a Reunion

When planning a reunion on a larger scale that is over fifty attendees you should allow about twenty-four months. The earlier you start planning your reunion, the more likely you are to have good attendance. In 2007, *Reunions Magazine* surveyed about 4,000 readers who were responsible for organizing their reunions. Almost 80 percent of the responses came from those who organized family reunions as opposed to class or military reunions. The result of the survey revealed that 68 percent of respondents reported that they had planned their reunions one year or longer ahead of the event and 21 percent had started planning two years in advance.

As you will learn later that summer months are popular for family reunions. Not only are they popular for reunions but they are also popular for weddings and conventions. Therefore, eighteen to twenty-four months will allow enough time to reserve hotel and banquet facilities.

Choosing the Reunion Date

The date you select for your reunion should be based on the results of your pre-reunion survey that was distributed in the initial planning stages of the reunion. Ideally, this survey should be sent out eighteen to twenty-four months prior to the proposed reunion date to allow enough time to plan your reunion. This time frame provides family members with enough time to submit vacation requests to their places of employment.

If you are asking yourself when do families generally plan their reunions, this question was answered in a survey conducted by Reunions Magazine in association with the Department of Hotel, Restaurant and Tourism Management, East Stroudsburg University of Pennsylvania (Source: http://www.reunionsmag.com/advertise/opportunities_research2.html). A random selection of Reunions Magazine readers received and responded to various questions including the month that they held their reunion. It was not surprising to learn that 85 percent of the respondents reported their family reunions occurred in June, July, and August. The summer months are usually ideal for planning a reunion since the children are out of school and this is when many people plan vacations from work.

Based on surveys that they have conducted over the years, Reunions Magazine offers several suggestions when considering a reunion date. Because families often plan even their summer vacations and holidays at least a year in advance, Reunion Magazine recommended that families allow at least two years before the target date. They suggest that reunion planners pitch out the idea when family members are already together for events such as a wedding, graduation, or holiday. Give everyone three or four specific dates or seasons to consider. Ask for theme or venue ideas. Then, after everyone has had a chance to check family and work calendars, send out "save the date" invitations to everyone involved. Set your first reunion date to draw as many people as possible. If the reunion is a new idea, distant members need to save both time and money for the trip. Additionally, it was suggested that you should consider choosing a reunion date that coincides with an important family event to generate more interest. For example, let say you know that you have an older aunt celebrating a milestone birthday (80th, 90th, and 100th) in the summer. Planning a family reunion around this event is likely to draw more people. I know in my family; family participation is usually greater when a special event is being celebrated that coincides with a reunion. Finally, offer choices with a commitment to abide by the consensus of the family. If after receiving the results of the pre-reunion survey you learn that the majority of the respondents request the reunion to be held in July, then this is the date that you should go with.

Type of Reunion to Host

(Source: http://www.familyreuniontips.com/html/reunion_type.htm)

Most reunions can be categorized into three basic types: a one-day event like a picnic or barbecue, a weekend event or week-long event. The easiest and least expensive type of reunion to host would be a picnic or barbecue at one of your relative's home or a nearby park. However, the focus of this book is family reunion planning on a larger scale.

I personally recommend hosting a weekend event as opposed to a week-long event since reunions held over three days are much more involved and costly. You will learn later that in a survey conducted by Reunions Magazine most people hold their reunions over two days. While three-day reunions do require some advanced planning of multiple events, lodging has to be dealt with and travel arrangements need to be made, and they can't be affordable for most families. I will address ways of keeping the cost of your reunion to a minimum even when planning larger scale reunions within the next few sections of this book.

How Long to Host the Reunion?

(Source: http://www.genealogy.com/genealogy/32_reunion.html)

The decision of how long to host your reunion should come from the results of the pre-reunion survey. Typically, most families plan a three-day weekend reunion. Three-day reunions are generally preferred for reasons previously mentioned. This information was supported in surveys published in Reunions Magazine. Over 70 percent of the respondents of the Reunions Magazine/East Stroudsburg University study reported that held their reunions for two or more days. Today many reunions start on Friday and last through Sunday, though some families may stay longer. One whole week is not unusual. If members travel long distance, a longer stay makes the effort worthwhile with time to visit and relax before the return journey.

Reunion Location

When choosing a location for your reunion, consider the ages, interests, convenience, and limitations of your family members. Is there a nearby shopping mall? What activities are there for children? Is there a pool for the teens? How accessible is it for all of your reunion activities? Hotels and resorts make hosting reunions easier. You can often block groups of rooms, enjoy discounted rates, and have the option of either working out your own activities or having the concierge to help you plan other activities.

I recommend hosting large reunions at either a hotel or a resort since they normally have all the facilities in-house for a successful weekend event. It makes sense to have your family members at a central location for the reunion. It could be the location for the welcoming/check-in table as well as the banquet, the worship service, and brunch.

Anytime you are planning an event that involves overnight accommodations and transportation, cost can start to add up. Keeping cost to a minimum should be a goal of every reunion planning and subcommittee member so that as many people as possible will be able to participate in the reunion.

There are ways that I have found to keep the cost of your reunion to a minimum, even when hosting your event at your hotel or resort of your choice. When my family hosts its out-of-state reunions, there are a number of ways in which we control cost. The first thing you should consider is renting a large van and have family members travel together, sharing the cost of the vehicle expenses. The same should be done with hotel rooms. Hotel chains such as the Holiday Inn, Embassy Suites, and Hyatt Regency are very family reunion friendly and generally charge an extra $10 per person for the third and fourth occupant in the room using existing beds. Paying an extra $10 or $20 per night is less expensive than the cost of another hotel room. Just keep in mind that the best hotel or resort to host your reunion will be the one that is the most affordable and meet your family's needs. You will definitely need to shop around to get the best deal.

As discussed earlier, hotel chains such as the Holiday Inn, Embassy Suites, and Hyatt Regency are very family reunion friendly, in my experience. These hotels chains are probably in most U.S. cities or towns, making them convenient for hosting reunions. Those of you considering hosting your reunion at a resort may consider the recommendations given by Hotel Club (Source: http://blog.hotelclub.com/family-reunion-resorts). They rated their top nine picks for resorts, if your family would like to venture out a little further. Their picks in order from one to nine respectively are as follows:

1. Lake Crescent Lodge—Olympic National Park, Washington, D.C

2. The Broadmoor—Colorado Springs, Colorado

3. Skytop Lodge—Skytop, Pennsylvania

4. The Moorings Village Resort—Islamorada, Florida

5. Congress Hall—Cape May, New Jersey

6. La Jolla Beach and Tennis Club—La Jolla, California

7. Sun Valley Resort—Sun Valley, Idaho

8. Hotel Iroquois—Mackinac Island, Michigan

9. Tides Inn—Chesapeake Bay, Virginia

Outside of cost, a convenient location is another prominent factor in choosing where to have your reunion. In fact, 20 percent of respondents from the Reunions Magazine/East Stroudsburg University study indicated that a convenient location was the most prominent factor in choosing where to have a reunion (Source: www.reunionsmag.com/advertise/opportunities_research2.html). Almost as many respondents cited reasonable lodging cost, reasonable travel cost, and availability of recreational activities. Other responses included the following: the same place every year, a variety of accommodations and activities, or shopping and destinations that match a theme. All families try to find special places ranging from their own backyard to historical family homesteads or even a dream locale. The reunions that hundreds of members meet more comfortably are in hotels, resorts, and even on cruise ships. The possibilities are infinite—smaller groups may be more comfortable at inns, ranches, condos, villas, bed and breakfasts, or campgrounds.

It's not unusual for a reunion group to choose a place they've not been to. Convention and visitors or tourism bureaus are eager to convince families to visit their areas. They offer a plethora of information including contacts with facilities and activities. Also when considering reunion locations, be sure to check out the directories of hundreds of reunion-friendly places in Reunions Magazine and Reunions Workbook. Many of the listings are just a click away with direct Internet links such as www.reunionsmag.com.

If you want to get your family's interest in the reunion and generate excitement among them, advance preparation is the key. Start by selecting the perfect location. Use of Internet technology is best way for you to search multiple reunion locations at the same time. You want to find a reunion location that is central so that every member of your family has an easy time getting there. You also want to make sure the location has enough attractions and things to do for all ages so that every member of the family, young and old, is excited about the trip.

When you send out invitations or announcements about the upcoming reunion, make sure you mention the features of your hotel or resort. The more you promote your reunion and all the things you have to offer, the more likely you will beget greater participation from across the board (Source: http://www.familylobby.com/family-tips/family-reunion.asp?id=53#tips and http://grouptravel.org/Family-Reunion/5-amenities-to-ask-for-when-blocking-hotel-rooms-for-a-family-reunion.html).

Hospitality and Lodging

Room Reservations

(Source: http://www.hotelplanner.com/Family-Reunion-Hotels/Family-Group-Hotels.html)

After choosing the date and location of your reunion, the first thing you must do is reserve rooms at a local hotel for your out-of-town guests. The worst thing that could happen is when your guests try to call around for a hotel room a few months before your family reunion, to only find out that all the rooms in town are $200 plus per room per night or even worse all rooms in town have all been taken by a large convention or sporting event. This is why it is very important to reserve a block of rooms for your guests at special rates at your hotel or resort well in advance of the big event. At most hotels and resorts, the minimum number of guests rooms required to make a block is 10 rooms per night. If you are looking for over 30 rooms per night, another good idea is to split the group blocks among two to three hotels. This way your guests can have a choice between different locations and prices.

To accomplish this goal, you do not want to start blindly calling hotels in multiple locations. You will not be doing your family or yourself any favors by reserving blocks at the first rates the hotel will quote. You also do not have all the information on the hotel, and it is important you get organized detailed descriptions of all amenities before you make any decisions. First step is to see what rates are out there on the Internet. A great source that I have found for easily comparing different hotel Internet rates is HotelPlanner.com (www.HotelPlanner.com). The best thing about their system is that it is free and very easy to use. All you need to do is put in your family reunion location options and dates and HotelPlanner.com will do the rest. It will allow you to search hotel group rates in multiple cities at the same time in a clear and organized approach without hotel bias. It also puts you in control of sorting through this information by location, price, or hotel brand names. They will also assign an account representative to you that will help make sure your hotel deals are not only the best, but they will help with the reservation process as well. The reservation process is very important because even if the room rate is very low, the deal may include a very strict cancellation policy, a high cash deposit, or other hidden costs such as mandatory resort fees. The HotelPlanner.com account representative will be more than happy to help through these and all of the other issues you may encounter. After choosing your hotel they will set up a special online booking Web site just for your family reunion, free of charge. This will help you keep track of your family members as they confirm with your hotel.

Concessions

Concessions are anything the hotel or resort is promising to give you in exchange for your business, either for free or at a discount (Source: Reunions Magazine, May/June/July 2011. Vol. 21, No 4, p.10). Concessions should be clearly documented with any associated costs in your contract. Typical concessions include a hospitality room, discounted-room rates, meals, and reduced-parking fees (Source: Reunions Magazine, May/June/July 2011. Vol. 21, No 4, p.10). When blocking thirty rooms or more, there are five concessions that you should negotiate with the hotel representative. This list was compiled from grouptravel.org and includes a free hospitality room, free shuttle to the local sopping/restaurant, free Internet, free breakfast, and a free hospitality room (Source: http://grouptravel.org/Family-Reunion/5-amenities-to-ask-for-when-blocking-hotel-rooms-for-a-family-reunion.html).

Free Hospitality Room or Suite

A hospitality room or suite is important to have when hosting your family reunion. This room provides a place for family to gather, mingle, catch up, share photos, pick up their registration packets, and chat in a private setting. The hospitality room becomes the go-to place at a hotel for all family reunion members instead of one's personal room. This is one concession that is very important to make sure you ask for, and that it is free. Hotels will generally give a free room or suite on the basis of how many actual rooms are reserved by the group. The ratio for most hotels is 1:30 which would mean that for every thirty rooms reserved and used by your family reunion, one room will be free. In most cases, the free room goes to the reunion planning committee chairperson or president. If your family falls short of the designated number of rooms to get a free room, then you should include this expense as part of the reunion fees. Don't forget to negotiate that the hospitality suite be cleaned daily by housekeeping staff (Source: http://www.familylobby.com/family-tips/family-reunion.asp?id=53#tips and (Source: http://www.familylobby.com/family-tips/family-reunion.asp?id=53#tips and http://grouptravel.org/Family-Reunion/5-amenities-to-ask-for-when-blocking-hotel-rooms-for-a-family-reunion.html).

The hospitality room should be available 24/7 with light refreshments and beverages for arriving guests. Reunion organizers should bring along or rent, computer, scanner, and copier to keep in the hospitality room to share photos, etc. The copier is essential for providing information on the last-minute changes to the program that was handed out when everybody arrived.

(Source: http://www.familylobby.com/family-tips/family-reunion.asp?id=53#tips)

The hospitality room can also be used as a game room especially for reunions lasting two or more days. It is a good idea to have a room available for downtime in between scheduled activities or in the event of inclement weather. It's a good idea to have several decks of playing cards, crossword puzzles, and board games for all ages. You might also provide a variety of magazines and newspapers for individual enjoyment. Set up tables with a different craft at each one. This is a fun thing for both kids and adults. They can go from station to station or just choose one craft they would like to make.

Free Shuttle Service

Hotel shuttle service is another important concession to negotiate. Shuttle service generally provides transportation to and from the airport and train and bus stations and may include rides to local shopping malls and restaurants. Providing transportation for a large group can be expensive and the hotel can save your family money by providing this service. If a hotel does not offer this free service, you should think twice about contracting with this facility. If the hotel where you have contracted a block of rooms does offer shuttle service, then it is not much of a stretch for them to provide a free ride for your family reunion attendees to a local shopping mall or even a restaurant. Lastly, if the hotel does agrees to provide the shuttle at little or no cost, make sure you tip the driver (Source: http://www.familylobby.com/family-tips/family-reunion.asp?id=53#tips and http://grouptravel.org/Family-Reunion/5-amenities-to-ask-for-when-blocking-hotel-rooms-for-a-family-reunion.html).

Free Internet

Free Wi-Fi is a must when contracting with your hotel of choice. Nowadays, many people travel with Wi-Fi___33 enabled devices such as laptops, tablet personal computers, and smart phones, allowing them to be able to connect to the Internet. The last thing you want your family members to do is to pay expensive hourly rates to log on to the Internet when many cafés and bars offer free Internet access (Source: http://www.familylobby.com/family-tips/family-reunion.asp?id=53#tips and http://grouptravel.org/Family-Reunion/5-amenities-to-ask-for-when-blocking-hotel-rooms-for-a-family-reunion.html).

Free breakfast

Pick a hotel that offers a free full hot breakfast to all its guests. This alone saves your family members at least $10-$15 per person per day. Depending on the size of your family reunion, that kind of savings can add up to a huge amount. If you insist on blocking rooms at a hotel that charges for its breakfast, then negotiating for it to be free will be a challenge. Only large family reunions will have enough buying power to be able to request free breakfast for all their attendees (Source: http://www.familylobby.com/family-tips/family-reunion.asp?id=53#tips and http://grouptravel.org/Family-Reunion/5-amenities-to-ask-for-when-blocking-hotel-rooms-for-a-family-reunion.html).

Reunion Theme

A theme is a defined as a unifying or dominant idea. While it is not necessary for your family to have a reunion theme, many families decide to do so. Themes are not only a source of inspiration; they serve as a guide and basis for the events activities. Themes require planning and advance announcements so that family members come prepared. Many themes have to do with history and some aspect of family tradition or heritage. They can be serious or fun but should involve everyone. Themes can also take on great significance as an opportunity to educate family members, particularly younger members, and the next generation who are expected to carry on the family reunion tradition.

There a number of creative themes for consideration. For example, you can have a theme that reflects your family's place of origin. At the reunion, you can select one or more days to have your family dress up in clothing from your place of origin. If your family shares African ancestry roots, consider having everyone dress up traditional African attire on the night of the banquet dinner. Make sure you plan meals, activities, and decorations around the theme.

Themes can also be celebrated in the form of a slogan or motto. Slogans and mottos are simply phrases that describe the general motivation or intention of the family. Many a time, families will have slogans or mottos placed on the reunion tee shirt. In my family's earlier reunions our motto or theme was "Reeder's On the Move." It later changed and remains, "Reeder's Joining Hands Across America." This motto describes our mission to connect with all across America. In addition to putting your slogan or motto on the reunion tee shirt, I recommend placing it on all the reunion literature especially the reunion souvenir booklet and welcome banner (Source: http://www.familylobby.com/family-tips/family-reunion.asp, http://grouptravel.org/Family-Reunion/family-reunion-budget-free-download.htm, l, http://familyreunionplanners.blogspot.com/2011/05/five-fun-family-reunion-themes.html, http://en.wikipedia.org/wiki/Slogan).

Reunion Souvenir Booklet

There should be a souvenir book or booklet at every reunion so that relatives have a keepsake to remember the reunion. You can keep the cost of preparing the booklet by doing most of the work yourself on a personal computer. The keepsake book tells a story about your family. The reunion booklet contents should be as follows: cover, chairperson's welcome letter, welcome from local public officials/dignitaries, family history, in memoriam section, outline of activities, dinner banquet menu and program, family business card, family address directory, and acknowledgments. This is not meant to be an all-inclusive list, but general guidelines on what can be included in your family reunion souvenir booklet.

Family Reunion Tee Shirt

(Source: http://www.ehow.com/how_4492180_plan-family-reunion-tshirt.html and http://www.aagsnc.org)

Family reunion tee shirts make a unifying statement at a family reunion picnic especially during the family picture. Custom tee shirts make a good family reunion souvenir and are relatively inexpensive. With some time and group effort, family members can save money by making family reunion tee shirts using these easy steps.

The design of your family's tee shirt should reflect the reunion themes, colors, and the branches of the family tree represented. Tee shirts should be prepaid with other reunion fees at least one month prior to the start of the reunion to allow the printer time to have them ready on first day of the reunion.

You can make your own family reunion tee shirts by developing a creative design. Many office supply or hobby stores sell thermal transfer paper, which you can print designs on and then iron onto a tee shirt. When you send out your invitations, you can determine how many people want to buy a family reunion tee shirt, and collect the funds with the other reunion fees. Buy plain white cotton tee shirts in bulk and figure their cost and the cost of the transfer paper. Or if you don't want to do all the work yourself, have someone print family reunion tee shirts for you.

I personally recommend that you locate an affordable tee shirt screen printer. You may find one in your area, or online. Often there are local companies who design custom tee shirts for community businesses. Sometimes they will give discount rates to family reunion projects, as a good will, public relations gesture, to gain future business on a larger commercial project.

When you talk to the screen printer, ask how they want the artwork or logo delivered for the shirt, and if there will be a setup fee. Delivery of the artwork may influence the total price. Often screen printers charge more for additional ink colors, so be clear with what you want, and how many colors you want on your shirt, when obtaining a price quote. Make sure the printer can deliver in time for the reunion. Design the logo. Remember to include the date of the event, family surname, and graphics that depict the location of the family reunion. Next prepare an order sheet for your family members. Include places to note the family member's name, size of shirt needed, and if a payment has been made. Take orders for the tee shirts after you know the prices, yet before you place the order with the screen printer. Remember to add in any shipping charges and sales tax that the printer may be charging you. Encourage family members to prepay for the shirts, before you place your order. Place your order with the screen printer and deliver the logo. Order a couple of large or extra-large shirts, for family members who may decide at the last minute they would like to purchase a shirt. You will use your inventory sheet to tell the printer how many shirts you need and in what sizes. Pick up the completed tee shirt order. At the reunion, pass out the tee shirts to the family members, using your inventory list, and noting on the list when a family member has received their shirts.

Budgeting and Finance

The finance committee is responsible for developing the family reunion budget. This committee is responsible for forecasting and budgeting and planning the income and expenses of the entire family reunion. If you have someone in your family who is an accountant or entrepreneur, this person may be a good candidate to head this committee. Someone who is familiar with balancing books and working with spreadsheets is the ideal person to make sure that costs don't get out of hand.

There are two free family reunion budget templates in Word, Excel, and PDF format. The first one is a simple budget that can be downloaded and changed to your needs. The other document is a Microsoft Excel spreadsheet that helps you figure out a cost per person for the reunion. You can find these budgets on the GroupTravel.org's Web site (Source: http://grouptravel.org/Family-Reunion/family-reunion-budget-free-download.html).

You may choose to finance your family reunion in a variety of ways. Depending on the type and length of your reunion, you could establish an overall budget and ask each family member to contribute a set amount based on dividing all expenses equally. This is the most common way. Many families have fundraising activities to help offset individual family reunion fee which can be both lucrative and fun (Source: http://www.hotelplanner.com/Family-Reunion-Hotels/Family-Group-Hotels.html).

Edith Wagner, Editor of Reunions Magazine, wrote an article on Genealogy.com's Web site on the topic of financing reunion fundraisers (Source: http://www.genealogy.com/46_reunion.html). Many of the fundraising ideas presented were from family reunion planners surveyed over the years. Some of the ideas shared I found to be useful information.

Before embarking on any fundraising effort, a bank or credit union account should be opened. This account should be set up requiring two people to sign for transactions. Opening a bank account for your family is a must, if you have a large number of people attending the reunion or if you are offering installment payments for reunion fees. The next step is to develop a detailed budget. Each reunion planning subcommittee head should submit a budget to the treasurer to present to the reunion planning committee for final approval. For example, if a van or bus rental is required, then the person heading the transportation committee should have a budget drafted up for these items. The reunion fees should be covered in your first reunion invitation letter in advance when requesting reunion fee payment.

Fundraiser Ideas

(Source: http://www.genealogy.com/46_reunion.html)

Family reunions can be costly but with careful planning every family can afford to have one. These costs may be passed on to the family members as part of their registration fee. The reunion planning committee should be aware that deposits might also be needed for the banquet sites, souvenirs, and printing materials. However, some families have fundraising events during the year to offset these expenses. Fundraisers may include dinner dances and parties, raffles, casinos or theater trips, card parties, flea markets, auctions, and any other way that people raise money.

Fundraisers that require even more time to plan and execute are long-term projects such as soliciting corporate support, decorating and making quilts, collecting recipes and producing cookbooks and many other publishing projects such as directories, scrapbooks, and history books. Advance planning is also required for ordering personalized (imprinted) products such as tee shirts, caps, coffee mugs, pens, pencils, and many more items.

Auctions are another method some families use to raise reunion funds. You can have each member bring something to auction off — artwork, crafts, baked goods, crafts, wood items, plants, quilts, purchased items, etc. Members who own businesses can donate professional services or products. Then you can invite others to join the auction to purchase these items (Source: http://www.temple.edu/fri/familyreunion/organize/finances.html and www.aagsnc.org/articles/relationships.html).

In sum, let's review the steps in financing a reunion. First, set is to develop a budget for all expense and then set the registration fee. Include a copy of the budget in early mailings. Request to open a free, temporary checking account in the name of your family reunion or chairperson's name. Keep reunion funds separate from personal funds. You can also consider a permanent account if you decide to establish a family association.

Family associations are legal entities that accept applications for membership. Generally, due are required annually or some family associations offer lifetime memberships for a set fee. Family associations must have Constitution and Bylaws. The mission, purpose, objectives, and membership requirements must be clearly stated. A board of directors is required. The proceeds of the family association's fund are generally for research, preserving family history documents and photos, and to finance communications such as Web sites, newsletters, etc.

Communications

Mailing Lists/Family Directory

Mailing lists and family directories are a great way to make sure everyone in the family stays in touch and are necessary when planning your reunion. They can be created and printed out quite easily using genealogy software packages as previously mentioned such as Legacy and RootsWeb. The family directory should be given to all of the attendees of the reunion as a gift. The communications committee is responsible for creating the directory. It doesn't have to be expensive, and you can make it right at home on your computer. To save on the cost of stationary and printing supplies, I would strongly recommend creating a Web site for your family therefore allowing everyone to have access to the directory online.

Invitations

Once you have completed a survey to determine the specifics of your reunion, then by the time you send your first invitation, the reunion will have come to no great surprise to anyone. As mentioned previously, the survey should be distributed eighteen to twenty-four months prior to the proposed reunion date. Nine months prior to your proposed date, some form of communications should be forwarded to family informing them to expect the first formal invitation with specific reunion details in the coming months. This will build up interest regarding the reunion and help your family spread the word to other relatives. I recommend sending the second formal invitation letter six months prior to the reunion date and the third and final letter three months before the reunion. You can refer to appendix A for sample letters. For those family members who have given their e-mail address, take advantage of technology and forward as many letters as possible via e-mail. This will cut down cost of stationary and postage. The communications committee has the responsibility of compiling and forwarding all reunion invitations. If you don't have a communications committee then the reunion planning committee should be responsible for this task.

Content of the Invitation Letter

There are some basic elements that your reunion invitation letter should contain. As with all other letters, you should start with the following:

- Date, time, and location of the reunion

- Chairperson's address, phone number, and e-mail address

- Cost per person or family and what is included in reunion fees

- Payment plan schedule. Who to make the check or money order out to.

- A preaddressed response card or form.

- Directions on how to get to the reunion venues and other activities

- Mention if the guests should bring along any special clothing or equipment. This is especially important you have a special reunion theme.

- Don't forget to inform your family to bring old family photos or albums. Photos can be displayed at any time during the reunion.

- Detailed description of activities and itinerary.

Following Up Letters

It's always a nice gesture if two weeks prior to the reunion to send a communication to family members as a reminder about things that they may forget. Include a list of things that they should bring to the reunion such as old photographs and family heirlooms to display. Let them know that you appreciate their attendance and participation in the reunion. You may consider writing something along these lines, "Thanks for your interest, can't wait to see you at the reunion" message at the end (Source: http://family-reunion.com).

Electronic Correspondence

Whether or not you mail out invitations, you may choose to send e-cards or electronic invitations. Sending reunion correspondence via e-mail will help you to better coordinate your reunion and keep everyone abreast of updates much quicker and less costly than traditional mail.

This can be as simple as sending e-mail messages to your family members. However, you can also use electronic postcards, i.e., e-cards, such as the free and easy family reunion e-cards. If you utilize the e-cards on the WikiTree Web site, they are free of charge and have no advertising or gimmicks. They are simple and classy (Source: http://www.wikitree.com/wiki/Space:Postcards).

Promoting Your Family Reunion

(Source: http://www.wikitree.com/articles/family-reunion-ideas.html#reunion-leadership and http://grouptravel.org/Class-Reunion/spreading-the-word-about-your-class-reunion.html

Once you have decided on all of the details including the date, time, location, and type of reunion you will be having, you are going to need to take some time to prepare to advertise your event. You must consider advertising the location where you are having your reunion. Whether you are phoning, e-mailing, or mailing out personal invitations or are going to be placing an advertisement in the newspaper, the more you advertise your reunion, usually the better the attendance.

There are a number of creative ways in which to advertise your reunion. Some are more traditional while others are not so traditional. We have discussed electronic communications such as e-mail and e-cards. Creating a private family Web site and utilization of social networking sites are other ways in which to advertise your reunion.

In chapter 5, you learned about the various Web sites available to advertise your reunion, so now let's examine social networking Web sites.

Social Networking

(Source: http://www.wikitree.com/articles/family-reunion-ideas.html#reunion-webpage)

Social networking sites can be a great organizational tool to supplement your family's Web site. If some of your family members use Facebook this is recommended, but other social networking sites may also be just as useful and more efficient if it's what your family's members are used to using. Facebook can help you organize simply by serving as a place to exchange private messages or "wall" posts. You can also create a Facebook group for your reunion and/or a Facebook event.

Facebook Group

Here's how to create a Facebook group. Start by clicking the groups icon on the toolbar at the very bottom of your page. It looks like two people standing next to each other. From the main groups page, click the "Create a New Group" button in the upper-right corner. From there you can invite family members to join the group.

Facebook Event

Creating a Facebook event works almost exactly the same way. Start by clicking the events icon on the bottom toolbar. It looks like a calendar. Then click the "Create a New Event" button.

Although this is more limited as a forum, it has the advantage of the calendar function and RSVPing, i.e., the people you invite can say whether they will be attending, maybe attending, or not attending the reunion.

Capturing the Memories

(Source: http://www.familylobby.com/family-tips/family-reunion.asp and http://www.ehow.com/how_5088847_plan-memorable-family-reunions.html#ixzz1D9UvYsSD)

You should definitely have a plan for taking pictures at your reunion and designate an official professional reunion photographer. Family reunions are full of wonderful events, so having pictures for keeping those memories alive is very important. Avoid choosing an amateur for this event and make sure you have a backup photographer as well. Designate one to three people to take pictures of the event, encouraging them to get both impromptu and posed shots of everyone there. At the end of your reunion, have the designated photographers get together and compare their photos scanning through them, weeding out duplicates, and bad shots. Individuals and families can then look through the pictures and decide which ones they want copies of. Make copies at the local developer or have digital copies sent to everyone via e-mail.

Reunion Check-In and Registration

The first day of the reunion sets the tone for the rest of the reunion. Your goal is to make everyone feel welcomed and this starts with check-in and registration. To better identify your reunion, hotel staff can assist you in selecting a location for your reunion signs. It is a good idea to have a welcome banner.

The hospitality committee is responsible for welcoming the guests to the reunion. They are the ones who will greet the quest at the registration table. They should perform duties relating to making family members feel at home. Other responsibilities include distributing all reunion materials and packets such as the souvenir booklets, goodie bags, name tags, etc.

Update Information

Use check-in and registration as an opportunity to update information on your family members. Have a designated table or notebook to update the family tree, birthdays, mailing, and e-mail addresses, phone numbers, anticipated graduation dates, anniversaries, places of employment, and special skills. This information can be used in all sorts of ways such as to complete the family directory, family group sheets/records, and to develop family trivia games.

Name Badges

(Source: http://www.family-reunion-success.com/printable-name-tags.html)

Typically, during reunions there will be family members meeting one another for the first time. For large reunions, name badges are a "must have." Name badges facilitate communication and allay anxiety from having to worry about not recognizing someone or not knowing or remembering a name.

There are several ways you can prepare name badges for your reunion. You can use your computer to print out name tags for all the attendees. Avery.com makes hanging name badges suspended from a convenient neck strap for hands-free identification. There are several advantages of using the hanging badges over the stick-on or pinned versions. First, they are very easy to take on and off when changing clothes. Unlike, the stick on or pinned version, the Hanging Badges rarely are lost. They're easy to make right from your desktop. Just complete a free template from avery.com and print with your inkjet or laser printer. Then insert your new badge into its durable, soft vinyl holder and attach the strap. In addition to the person's name, you could add the city and state they live in. You can get creative and have a special color for each family branch. Name badge should be handed out as the family members arrive at the reunion during check-in and registration. It is important that attendees wear their badges throughout the reunion as a sign of unity. Be sure to bring extras, plus paper and scissors so you can easily whip up name hangers for unexpected guests.

Souvenirs and Giveaways

(Source: http://www.familylobby.com/family-tips/family-reunion.asp).

Family members look forward to receiving gifts and mementos during the reunion. There are three categories of gifts that you will want to include in your goodie bags. The first category is the required items pertinent to reunion and planned activities including name tags, family directory, maps, visitor's guides, brochures for local businesses, coupons for local attractions, agenda, etc. Consider providing water bottles for every family member at your reunion. You can even have them printed with your family name or crest.

Use a permanent marker to write each person's name on their own bottle and encourage family members to conserve paper cups and disposable plastic water bottles by refilling their personal bottle as needed. They'll help protect the environment and go home with a neat souvenir.

The next category includes general mementos that are not necessary for your reunion but just adds a nice touch. Some items to consider are pocket calendars/planners, mini hand sanitizer, facial tissue packets, mini flashlights, candy, plastic mugs, coasters, key rings, and writing pens. These gifts and souvenirs do not have to be costly and should be covered in the reunion fee. You should keep the cost of each item below a few dollars. Don't forget to also check with your local visitors and convention bureaus. They often have giveaway items. Your local Dollar Store will likely have plenty of items to choose from.

The third category of includes special family souvenirs. Items that you may want to consider are personalized sun visors, baseball caps, picture frames, etc. An endless variety of specialized products are available to commemorate your reunion. Catalogs are abounding with many possibilities and you'll want to explore lots of them. Just make sure you allow enough time for imprinted items to be completed before the reunion. I would allow at least six to eight weeks for completing the order before the reunion. It's important to note that some companies demand payment up front. Others accept orders payable by invoice. One last point, make sure you choose items that can be enjoyed by both males and females.

Planning Family Reunion Activities

Family members do look forward to having fun together. The range of possible activities is limitless. The more family members are involved in carrying out the activities, the more likely their participation will be over time. This is a time when talents in the family have an opportunity to shine. Use the abilities and interests of family members to have such activities as: talent shows, family history telling, choir singing, recognition ceremonies, arts and crafts exhibits, fashion shows, sports, music, and poetry.

A great starting point for planning your family reunion activities is to contact the local visitors and convention bureau. They can assist your family in planning events in your host city such dinning, entertainment, tours of historic sites, museums, sightseeing, nightlife, special events, and many other attractions. Often times they will provide you with discounts and coupons for many of these events.

Planning Tools

It's smart to invest in a specialized computer program to help you to organize and plan your reunion. The software is inexpensive and easy to install and, depending on the program you choose, might include spreadsheets, charts, or checklists to keep you organized, as well as templates for invitations, signage, and more. We will mention the three most popular reunion planning tools: family reunion organizer, reunion planner, and Fimark's family reunion planner. It's also a great idea to set up a family Web site early on. FamilyReunion.com and FamilyDetails.com are good places for beginners to start. Some formats allow you to update event information, share lodging suggestions, tally RSVPs, e-mail reminders, and even share pictures and videos (Source: http://www.womansday.com/Articles/Family-Lifestyle/How-to-Plan-a-Family-Reunion.html).

Family members may lead workshops in topics with which they

are familiar, such as economic development, investing, education, parenting skills, political action, etc. Remember to include activities for all ages, including the youth and the elderly (Source: http://www.temple.edu/fri/familyreunion/organize/activities.html).

Even if all the attendees know each other, it's still a good idea to plan activities that promote unity and bonding. The Web site FamilyReunion.com has almost a dozen activity suggestions. From there, try a few simple games: tug-of-war, relay races, sack races, or a scavenger hunt. But you don't need to have something scheduled for every minute. Give people some downtime, especially if you've picked a site with built-in activities, such as a campground with a lake. Find out ahead of time if your site has sporting equipment you can borrow or rent. It's a good idea, however, to bring everyone together toward the end of your reunion to watch old family movies or a slideshow (Source: http://www.womansday.com/Articles/Family-Lifestyle/How-to-Plan-a-Family-Reunion.html).

Day One Reunion Activities

(Source: http://www.wikitree.com/articles/family-reunion-ideas.html#reunion-webpage and http://family-reunion.com/ideas.htm and http://www.familylobby.com/family-tips/family-reunion.asp)

Reunion activities serve several purposes to help family become better acquainted and develop new relationships, to have fun, and share the family's history. During your reunion planning meetings, you should have organized subcommittees to carry out the various reunion activities. I have found that most families follow a standard format with regards to reunion activities. For example, many families start their reunion off with registration and check-in followed by a "get acquainted night." The second day may include a picnic, city tour, banquet dinner, and dance. In consideration of family members returning home on the last day of a three-day reunion, activities are planned through early afternoon. Usually, a buffet breakfast or brunch will cap off many reunions. In the next few sections we will organize the various reunion activities based on a three-day event. When planning reunions on a larger scale it is best to limit your reunion activities to three days. This will help to keep your reunion affordable for everyone. So let's examine the various reunion activities as they are outlined and categorized by the day of the reunion.

The first day of arrival serves as a way for family to become reacquainted, reconnect, and establish new relationships. As mentioned previously, the first day of the reunion sets the tone for the rest of the reunion.

Get Acquainted Night

Depending on how many rooms have been reserved for your family, some hotels offer a free hospitality suite or smaller conference room. Based on the size of the room and number of attendees in your family group, the hospitality suite or conference room is an excellent location for your "Get Acquainted Night." Generally, our family starts this event at 6:00 p.m., allowing enough time for relatives to arrive by car, plan, train, or bus.

If your family reunion is going to be a large one with distant relatives who haven't seen each other in a while, you may need to plan for introductions. Provide name tags to be worn throughout the event. Lanyards with plastic name tag holders work well if you'll be meeting for several days or having outdoor activities. You might even put additional information on the tags, such as hometown or family branch.

Plan some icebreakers to help distant cousins get to know each other. Encourage each individual family to bring a filled photo album to put on a designated table so everyone can see what they've been up to.

Set out a guest book for everyone to sign in on. Have them list their names, address, phone number and e-mail so you can keep the files and their information up to date for future news and contact?

Logo Contest

The goal of this contest is to have everyone at the reunion vote on a logo to be used for future reunions. And the winning individual will be announced during the reunion events. There are two ways you could obtain the drawings they choose from. The first is when invitations are sent out, you can include the announcement and have people send their drawings to the committee; in this way you can have all the drawings you receive printed up so they end up being the same size for display at the reunion. Second, you can announce the contest in the welcome packet and provide paper and markers for anyone who wants to draw a logo for the contest at the reunion.

Welcome Address

(Source: http://family-reunion.com/ideas.htm)

Whether your reunion is large or small, it's nice to have a "welcoming address" to kick the thing off. It doesn't have to be a long speech; five to ten minutes will suffice unless you have a really good speaker in the family. Here are a few things you might put in a welcoming address:

- Welcome everyone to the reunion, and thank them for coming.

- Mention which different families (or family lines) are at the reunion.

- Give a general outline of the weekend's activities.

- Thank the people who helped put the reunion together.

- And of course, add a few well-placed jokes or inspirational thoughts.

You can also use this time as an opportunity to give credit to the organizers. You might also want to list some of the people that are attending. You can recognize certain individuals or families that have traveled from far away or who might be less familiar. This can be a good way to go around the room and have individual to introduce to each other.

Consider inviting one or two local city officials such as the mayor or council members to give a formal welcome at your reunion. If the mayor or city council members are unable to attend the reunion, they may be willing to write a proclamation in honor of your family reunion. When our family hosted our reunion in the city of Atlanta, Georgia we were able to get the mayor to send us his photo and write a congratulatory letter that we included in our souvenir booklet.

You can send out press releases to the local newspaper and TV news networks to draw wider attention to your family reunion. Who knows, you may be able to get your family reunion highlighted on a local news network.

Quiz of Family History

This is an attention-getter to draw in people who have not thought family history was interesting. Use it when you want the group to quiet down and get ready for announcements, or for the central event, etc. To prepare for the quiz, you have to find some interesting facts about individuals. The quiz is a basic matching quiz, used widely in schools but works as a family reunion activity. On one side of a sheet of paper is a column with sentences such as those given above, numbered 1, 2, 3 etc. On the other side is a column of names, listed with a letter next to each. If you can find five sentences to put on the list, that's a good start, but ten would be better. Have people work on the quiz however they want, individually or with others, and after five minutes or so, read out the correct answers to them.

Day Two Reunion Activities

As mentioned previously, day one activities of your reunion are primarily centered on making your family feel welcomed. Keep in mind that most family members will be just arriving on day one, so keep your activities simple to give everyone an opportunity to rest up. Day two activities, on the other hand, should be focused on everyone getting reacquainted. The best way to do this is to plan structured icebreaker games as well as other activities to help your family to bond with one another.

Morning Activities

Family Picnic

(Source: http://www.familyreuniontips.com/html/picnic.htm)

The family picnic is probably the most popular activity planned at family reunions. When planning family reunions on a larger scale (fifty or more attendees), my recommendation is that you will want to have the event catered at the picnic grounds.

Picnic Location

Any city, state, or national park can be an excellent choice for a family reunion picnic. While they are usually equipped with picnic tables, public restrooms, and playgrounds, you'll probably want to bring extra chairs, blankets, and recreational equipment if you decide to go this route. Also make sure you have a first aid kit, insect repellant, sunscreen, hand sanitizing gel, wet wipes, paper towels, and trash bags.

When selecting a picnic site, look for the following amenities:

- Picnic tables
- Covered area in case of rain
- Free parking
- Public toilets
- Grills
- Playgrounds for the kids
- Recreational facilities (basketball courts, softball fields, volleyball, etc.)
- Easy to find location

Decorations

If you want to give your reunion a festive look and make your event even more exciting and memorable, decorations are the way to go. One way to make you picnic stand out from others who may be having a picnic at the same time is to create a banner with your family's name. This will help family members in locating your reunion. Use of balloons, flags, streamers, torches, and candles to put the finishing touches on your reunion site.

Picnic Activities

It's good to have lots of activities and games planned and available for reunion attendees. Because you will have relatives of all ages, from babies to senior citizens, we suggest activities that appeal to all age groups. Activities you may want to consider include: softball, basketball, volleyball, water balloon toss, three-legged races, horseshoes, Frisbee, kickball, family relay races, tug-of-war, and DJ music and dancing.

For young children over the age of five, you should have activities specifically for them like face painting, jump rope, piñata, hula hoops, and scavenger hunts. Moonbounces are usually a hit with the kids. The come in a variety of sizes and many themes for a rental fee. Giant water slide would be a great idea if you picnic facility does not have a pool or is not located near a water body.

If you are selecting a picnic site at a public park, picnic ground or forest preserve, you will probably need a permit for a particular spot and date. Make sure you have your permit before you finalize the reunion date.

City or Town Tour

Popular U.S. cities are excellent places to host reunions. Our family has hosted reunions in Atlanta, Tampa, Charlotte, Philadelphia, and Washington, DC. Our first national reunion back in 1993 was held in Philadelphia, Pennsylvania. What made Philadelphia an excellent city to host our reunion was all that it had to offer. Philadelphia is the second largest city on the east coast and ranks sixth in the nation, with a metropolitan population of over 5 million. Philadelphia is conveniently located in the middle of the northeast corridor, 100 miles south of New York, 133 miles north of Washington, D.C., and 55 miles from Atlantic City. More than 63 million people—approximately a quarter of the U.S. population—live within a five and a half-hour drive from Philadelphia.

Philadelphia is accessible by car, train, bus, airplane, and even cruise ship. Our reunion was held at the Holiday Inn, which was within walking distance of the historic sites in Center City. The Philadelphia International Airport (PHL) is located approximately seven miles from Center City and serves more than twenty-five airlines. PHL is served by all major domestic carriers and is a major hub for U.S. Airways. The New International Terminal features thirteen new international gates and fifty-six U.S. immigration booths.

SEPTA's (Southeastern Pennsylvania Transportation Authority) Airport Line directly links the airport to Philadelphia's downtown for a fast, hassle-free connection. Philadelphia taxis charge a flat rate of $25 for travel between Center City and the airport.

Philadelphia is also served by Amtrak, which operates rail service along the northeast corridor stretching from Boston to Washington, and other major cities in the United States and Canada. Amtrak's 30th Street Station is minutes from the Pennsylvania Convention Center and Center City hotels.

Bus service to and from Philadelphia is excellent, with daily arrivals from all parts of the country. The Greyhound bus terminal is located in Center City and offers state of the art buses for travel to and from Philadelphia. Also, Greyhound is offering reduced fares from New York City to Philadelphia, if you book at least three days in advance.

The city tour is an activity that is generally well attended by most family members. This is not recommended for elder, frail individuals, unless a wheelchair is available.

For some, it may be the first time in the host city and people like to know what the respective city is known for in the area of its history, culture, entertainment, and famous people of origin. Philadelphia is the fifth largest city in the country, and it is filled with historic sites. Millions of people come to Philadelphia each year to visit Independence National Historical Park that has the greatest concentration of American history, including the Liberty Bell and Independence Hall. Philadelphia has new and one-of-a-kind attractions, a wealth of art and culture, renowned performing arts companies, distinctive architecture, a walkable downtown, seemingly endless shopping, and great restaurants.

Philadelphia is the birthplace of Declaration of Independence which was signed in 1776 and houses the famous Liberty Bell. Philadelphia has the first hospital. Step back in time to see where the Declaration of Independence and the U. S. Constitution were created.

Because there is so much to see in Philadelphia, the most popular tour is the Philadelphia Trolley Tour, because you can hop on and hop off the trolley at eighteen different stops throughout the city. Philadelphia is a great city for walking tours, too. If you have only a day, they also offer horse carriage tours, double-decker bus tours, helicopter tours, and many other ways to see the sights.

Don't miss the Philadelphia's sights from the water. See the sights, have a delicious meal, and enjoy the entertainment on a Philadelphia Dinner and Lunch Cruise. Just as a word of advice, when coordinating city tours. These tours should be planned early in the morning—between 9:00 and 10:00 a.m. to allow enough downtime for family to venture out and explore the city on their own. Usually there are a few who will want to shop or eat lunch at one of the famous eateries. Most reunions on large scale are held for three days. However, there may be family members that stay over a few days, later. The planning committee should make sure they have a list of activities of interest for these folks. This is usually the case for family members who drive to the reunion. You may want to suggest activities just outside of the city borders.

Just forty miles outside of Philadelphia is the Amish Country in Lancaster County, Pennsylvania. This is area is known to be one of the oldest and largest Amish Communities in America, a place where time stands still.

For those who prefer not to drive to Lancaster County, round-trip transportation can easily be arranged from many Center City hotels to Amtrak's Thirtieth Street Station. This historic train station is where the Harrison Ford movie, The Witness, was filmed. Upon arrival in Lancaster you will travel to the Amish Experience tour center, to spend a fun-filled day of sightseeing, shopping, and tasting delectable home-style cooking. View Jacob's Choice the Amish Experience F/X Theatre presentation. Take a guided tour of an Amish Country homestead. Take a leisurely trip through the back roads on a motor coach tour of Lancaster. Included on the tour are stops at an Amish quilt shop and bakery.

Children's Museum (ages 0-3 years)

(Source: http://www.visitphilly.com/museums-attractions/philadelphia/the-franklin-institute)

In Philadelphia there are several museums specifically designed for children. First, is the Please Touch Museum. Please Touch Museum is home to six interactive exhibit zones across 38,000 square feet, designed to encourage learning through play. Let your child be your guide as you explore our unique environment. The open-endedness of our unique exhibits allows families to personalize each visit, for there is no wrong way to play! It is designed for children of ages three and younger.

Academy of Natural Science

Founded in 1812, The Academy of Natural Sciences is the oldest continually operating museum of its kind in the western hemisphere. It is one of the world's foremost natural history museums, sponsored some of the seminal explorations for American wildlife and fossils, and by the early 1900s, expanded those explorations to Africa, Asia, and the Antarctic. Researchers worldwide utilize the museum's more than 17 million specimens for biodiversity studies.

The discoveries that rocked the world then and now share four floors of exhibit space in this family-friendly museum that showcases the Academy's remarkable collections. The fully constructed Tyrannosaurus rex, one of the largest meat-eating dinosaurs, towers over Dinosaur Hall, also home to fossils of the Hadrosaurus foulkii, discovered in New Jersey in 1856. You can climb inside a Tyrannosaurus rex's skull, try on horns and claws, and dig for fossils.

Multitudes of butterflies from Kenya, Costa Rica, and Malaysia flit around you in a simulated tropical rain forest. Large game animals acquired in the 1920s and 1930s are mounted in 3-D painted dioramas that replicate their natural habitats; for Philadelphians of that era, this was their first sighting of an Indian tiger or a wild beast.

Many of the museum's live animals are featured in shows throughout the day. Don't miss the small but dazzling gem and crystal collection.

In the Outside-In hands-on nature center, children can touch a hissing Madagascar cockroach or a snake, crawl through a tree trunk, and examine fossils under a microscope.

Franklin Institute Museum

In 1824, The Franklin Institute opened in Independence Hall to honor Benjamin Franklin and his inventiveness. In 1934, with the construction of the current building and the adjacent Fels Planetarium, it became a hands-on science museum. The IMAX Theater and the Mandell Center were added in 1990. Today, it's Pennsylvania's most-visited museum. In the museum's rotunda is the Benjamin Franklin National Memorial, with a twenty-foot-tall marble statue of the scientist and Founding Father.

An innovator in designing hands-on exhibits before "interactive" became a buzzword; the Franklin Institute is as clever as its namesake. Its eminently touchable attractions explore science in disciplines ranging from sports to space.

Highlights include The Sports Challenge, which uses virtual-reality technology to illustrate the physics of sports, The Train Factory's climb-aboard steam engine, Space Command's simulated earth-orbit research station, a fully equipped weather station, and exhibits on electricity.

Films like Everest and The Lion King assume grand proportions on the Tuttleman IMAX Theater's seventy-nine-foot domed screen. Galaxies are formed and deep space explored in North America's second-oldest planetarium, which reopened in 2002, sporting the continent's most advanced technology. Don't miss the 3-D theater and the indoor SkyBike.

Another unique feature of the Franklin Institute is that houses a giant replica of the human heart. You are able to walk through the heart, which is 15,000 times life size, like a human corpuscle. This is one of the museum's first and most popular attractions.

So, whatever city you choose to host your reunion just keep in mind that people want to see what's unique and different in that city or town. Showcase special activities that make their experience memorable.

Downtime

If your family reunion will last for more than one day, be sure to include some downtime in the schedule. Family members tend to get a little testy, if every moment is planned for them and they are required to participate in something round the clock. A week-long reunion may even require a "day off" in the middle of the week when individuals, family units, or couples can plan their own activities. Give family members the freedom to opt out of an activity or two. You might prefer they all participate in everything, but in the long run it's better to have everyone happy and cooperative.

Evening Activities

Icebreaker Games

Many times when families first come together, after a year or more of being apart, they feel a little timid until they get reacquainted with everyone. Icebreaker games are designed to create a welcoming, open atmosphere and can really accelerate the process of getting reacquainted with each other. They are an excellent way to learn the names and interests of family members. Keeping in mind that the purpose of your reunion is to rekindle old relationships and connect with new relatives, this section presents activities that create a positive-group atmosphere, help people to relax, and break down social barriers.

There are some "Do's and Don'ts" when planning icebreaker games. First, do not plan games that will make others uncomfortable, physically or mentally. You should avoid games that result in family members feeling embarrassed or like a fool. Only choose games that help your family members feel welcome and comfortable at your family reunion. Don't limit ice breaker games to the beginning of the reunion, use them to revitalize the group at any time. In this section, we will review in detail some of the more popular icebreaker games. Our family have played a few of these games and had a great time doing so (Source: http://familyreunionhelper.com/blog/2010/03/really-cool-ice-breaker-games).

Family Trivia Bingo

(Source: Share Did You Know? Bingo on your Web site or blog! Copy and paste the URL: http://www.icebreakers.ws/large-group/did-you-know-bingo.html)

This is one of my personal favorites. I love this game because it is very interactive and requires family members to go from table to table or group to group to find out what they have in common with each other. This game (also known as the autograph game) also helps individuals to learn interesting facts about each other. People walk around the room and mingle until they find people that match the facts listed on a bingo-style sheet. This game is a get-to-know-you style icebreaker. The recommended group size is over thirty people and it is for those aged twelve and up. It can be played indoors or outdoors. Materials required are: printed bingo sheets or card and pens.

We played this game on the second evening of our reunion after eating dinner in the hotel's banquet room. The best person to organize this game is the family historian, who has complied interesting facts about the family. My cousin Deborah Scott, one of our family's historians compiled facts about individual relatives from the family group sheets and other sources. Some the facts that were collected included the following: favorite color, family members who served in the military, birthday in the same month, family member who attended all reunions, those who have same number of children, those who live in same state, married same number of years, just to name a few. The Web site www.uncommoncourtesy.com has preprinted FamilyTriviaBingo cards that you can purchase, if you choose not to make your own cards (Source: http://www.uncommoncourtesy.com/FamilyTriviaBingo.htm).

The objective of this game is for people to wander around the room and to obtain the signatures of people who have the facts listed on the bingo sheet. Once a person successfully obtains a full row (five in a row), whether horizontally, vertically, or diagonally, he or she shouts "Bingo!" and wins.

This game requires a little bit of setup. Prepare a five by five table, with interesting facts written inside the boxes. Be creative! You can mark the center square "Free Space" like traditional bingo games. After you have prepared the table, print out enough copies for the number of players you are expecting.

Instructions on how to play this game is given in detail. First, pass out a sheet to each person, along with a pen. Explain the objective of the game and the following rules: (1) each person you talk to may only sign your sheet once, and (2) to win, you must get signatures to form five in a row horizontally, vertically, or diagonally. Say "Go!" and ask your participants to begin. When playing games or doing challenges, separate teams by birth months. That way they all have something to talk about in comparing their birthdates and can bond.

Once someone shouts "Bingo!" everyone returns and the person must introduce the people who signed his or her sheet. If desired, you can ask each person to explain their facts. This game is a fun way to get to know humorous or unique facts about your family.

"I've Never" Game

(Source: http://www.familylobby.com/family-tips/family-reunion.asp)

"I've Never" is a good icebreaker game to help everyone get reacquainted and is fun to play. You start by getting all of your family in a large circle and give each person ten pennies. Instruct the first person to announce something to the group that he or she has never done (truthfully). Everyone in the circle who has done that thing must now give that person one penny. For instance, Cousin Bill announces that he has never baked a cake, everyone in the circle who has never baked a cake would hand over one of their pennies him. Everyone who has baked a cake is safe. Now the next person in the circle announces something he or she has never done and the game continues. The game can last as long as you desire. Depending on how many of your family members who participate, you might want to end the game after everyone has had one, two, or three turns to name something they have never done. The person with the most pennies at the end of the game wins!

Other Evening Activities

Baby Photo Guessing Game

Have everyone bring a baby picture and post them all up on a wall with a number. Have everyone write down their guesses as to who is who and then check the correct answers to see who got the most right. The person who gets the most right wins a prize.

Display Works of Art

Displaying the achievements of family members is another activity to support your reunion goals; however, a cautionary note: it can really only be done inside, and, if it is in a hotel or other similar facility, it has to be done inside a room which can be locked when not in use (or, just have the display for a few hours and then take it down). If you have planned for a "gathering room" that would be a good place. Talented family members who have created paintings, books, crafts, etc., might think it out of place to bring along their stuff to show at a reunion. But this is an open invitation, a friendly way for family members to get to know another side. Make it clear it's not a sale (although if a private conversation between two people lead to a sale, that's fine).

Family History Presentation

Almost everyone at the reunion will share a common interest in your family history and tree. This makes family history a fun activity for the reunion and a wonderful opportunity for the family historian or genealogists to collect information. In chapter 5, the various ways in which to present your family's history at the reunion was discussed such as PowerPoint presentation, family tree poster, and DVD movie.

Storytelling

Be sure to designate some time at your reunion for family members to tell stories about the past. Insist that the younger generations stick close for this activity. To keep their interest, you might even encourage them to put together a skit about one of the stories they hear. Offer a prize for the best skit.

Skits

(Source: http://www.organizeafamilyreunion.com/family-history-skits.html)

A family history skit can help you learn about your family heritage and help you discover who you really are. You can preserve your heritage and share history with everyone at your family reunion with a skit performed by several members of your family. Need ideas for your skit?

Start by talking to your family. Ask your grandparents, aunts, and uncles for stories and knowledge about your heritage.

When you interview relatives you can learn what their life was like before you were even born. You can ask open-ended questions about who, what, where, and when. I would highly recommend getting permission to use an audio and/or video recorder. That way you won't have a hard time remembering the juicy details. You can easily create a family reunion theme with ideas from your family history skit.

Below are a few questions that can help get you started with interviewing your relatives.

1. What did your parents do for a living?

2. Did you know your great-grandparents and what were their names?

3. Where did they live?

4. What do you remember the most about your childhood?

5. Did your family have any yearly special traditions?

6. What did you do for fun when you were young?

7. Where did you go to school?

8. What was your favorite subject?

9. When were you born?

10. When did you marry?

11. Who were your cousins?

12. Who were you aunts and uncles?

13. Tell me more about them and their personalities.

Questioning people in a group sometimes carry the conversations farther. The perfect place to get elder family members involved in a conversation is at a family reunion. Be sure to listen and take lots of notes. People love to talk about themselves and your relatives probably have a lot of fun and exciting memories to share. Get lots of creative ideas with copies of photos that display clothes, cars, etc., that can tell you a lot about your heritage.

Family History Theme

Your family history theme can be all about your family heritage. You can perform reenactments of what life was like when your grandparents or great-grand-parents were young. You can demonstrate how they cooked meals over a large black kettle outside in the yard or how they slept on hay mattresses. Another idea is to simply tell the life story of one of your family members in their own words. You will be surprised at how the younger children of your family enjoy playing such roles at the family reunion.

Health Education

Take the opportunity during your family gathering to talk about your family's health history. The National Kidney Disease Education Program has put together a downloadable guide to discussing family health specifically during African American family reunions. You can download all or specific portions of the guide at www.nkdep.nih.gov/familyreunion/guide.htm. You can also order a free hard copy of The Family Reunion Health Guide at this Web site.

Family History and Research Table

The family historian or genealogical researcher should definitely have a table set up at the reunion to display all their findings. You can display the family tree, old photos, interesting documents, and scrapbooks. If there are photos with unidentified people in them, this might be a good opportunity for other family members to fill in the gaps.

At our last reunion, I had a table displayed with the findings of the DNA test that was performed. I shared information about my great-great-grandparents' heritage. My great-great-grandmother had origins in Nigeria, Africa, but later settled in Ethiopia. Conversely, my great-great-grandfather was reported to be a Cherokee Indian with origins in Newberry, South Carolina. On the family history display table, I had information about the history of

Cherokee Indians and Hausa-Fulani Tribe obtained from findings of the DNA test.

During this reunion, we launched our family's new Web site. I brought along my laptop and was able to give a brief talk to family members, on how to sign-up and navigate the Web site. These are just a few examples of creative ways to make your family's history come alive.

Banquet Dinner

(Source: http://www.superpages.com/supertips/banquet-dinner.html and http://www.allampkin.com/BanquetInfo.pdf)

A banquet dinner consists of several different things working together to make the occasion an enjoyable one for your family. The dinner is just one portion of the banquet and can be either in buffet style or table service. Other things that you need to take into consideration are the budget, entertainment, rental equipment, agenda, and menu. When determining the steps you should take to organize a banquet dinner, it can be helpful to know some of the aspects involved in such a dinner.

The first step is confirming your date with the caterers or facility. This is one of the main reasons that you should start planning your reunion eighteen to twenty-four months in advance of the proposed date. During the summer months, many hotels host weddings and business conferences that may compete with your reunion. Starting this far in advance will give you the best chance in getting the facility and date you desire.

Once your date has been locked in, you must now determine your budget. There are many factors in determining a budget. First is the number of attendees and how much everyone is willing to pay.

This information can be obtained from the pre-reunion survey.

As far as location goes, most families choose to host their reunion banquet dinner at the same hotel where they are staying. However, this may not be financially feasible for everyone. If not, try to find an "all-you-can-eat" buffet in the city or town that you host your reunion and rent out a private room. This is a much cheaper option than renting out banquet facilities at a hotel. As a note, the facility may ask you for a deposit and guarantee in advance. You will have to pay for hundred dinners even if only seventy-five show up. Generally, a facility is prepared to serve about 10 percent more people than you guarantee. So it makes sense to guarantee a lesser number than you expect. Even some of those who told you absolutely they would be there, maybe even gave you a deposit; don't show for one reason or another. Just to be on the safer side, based on hundred projected attendees, I would guarantee the restaurant eighty-five; then you can always adjust your estimate. However, you should still ask the facility about their requirements in regard to a change in the guarantee.

Rental Equipment

You also have to talk with the facility about rental equipment that you may need such as a microphone, podium, head table, risers, piano, dance floor, etc.

Agenda

A typical agenda is as follows:

6:00 p.m.-7:00 p.m.—Social or cocktail hour

7:00 p.m.-8:00 p.m.—Dinner

8:00 p.m.-8:15 p.m.—Awards

8:15 p.m.- 9:00 p.m. — Entertainment/games

9:00 p.m.-9:10 p.m. — Raffle/door prizes

9:10 p.m.-1:00 a.m. — Dance

Having an hour to mingle is always a good idea. You and the family, both, will want everyone to be present when you actually sit down to eat. It's been my experience that almost everything starts late, so plan for it and don't be disappointed when it happens.

The cocktail hour can have a few luxuries, if the budget permits. A "hosted" bar means that drinks are free to the party-goers. Usually most families have a "no-host" bar, which means that everyone pays for his own drinks.

Another luxury would be hors d'oeuvres. Ask the facility how much they would cost. Don't be surprised if less costly fresh vegetables, like celery, carrots, broccoli, with a dip can be served. If you add in shrimp cocktail, the cost skyrockets.

Generally, everyone will have some form of entertainment during the cocktail hour. The facility may have music piped in through its sound system, which is certainly the most economical; however, for around $300 you could have live music. Most banquet facilities have a piano, sometimes on wheels, and will let you either rent the piano or use it for free. Fee for the piano rental should be from $50 to $100 and a piano player, anywhere from $150 to $250.

Dinner

If you have arranged for assigned seating, the facility will probably have numbered signs that can be placed on each table. If not, you'll have to make your own. Your guests can either learn the number of their table when they arrive or it could be written on their tickets in advance.

Opening

The reunion planning committee chairperson or president should step up to the microphone and announce that dinner is ready and ask everyone to take a seat. When this has been accomplished, he or she should welcome everyone.

It is appropriate at most banquets, to have someone give a blessing over the food. Individuals that you choose for these tasks should be asked in advance and their names and responsibilities should be listed on the printed on the program agenda, if there is one.

The Program

Following the prayer, your master or mistress of ceremonies should introduce everyone who will participate in the evening's events. After the brief opening ceremony, your moderator can tell everyone to enjoy their dinner! If you have some sort of music during the cocktail hour, you might consider having it continue through dinner.

Following the opening remarks, you should plan the evening's entertainment. This should be the highlight of the evening. This is a good time for icebreaker games and other activities that I will discuss in detail starting with the family talent show.

Family Talent Show

(Source: http://www.familylobby.com/family-tips/family-reunion.asp?id=8#tips)

A talent show consists of short two-to-five-minute performances by family members. At the end of the performances the contestants are judged by other family members or special judges and the winner is crowned champion and wins a prize.

If you're planning to have a family talent show during your reunion, make sure you have some necessary supplies on hand. A portable sound system, keyboard, and CD player will make your event look professional. Make sure you give everyone ample opportunity to prepare for their talent and bring the necessary props.

Group Photos

Throughout your reunion, the photographer will be taking pictures, highlighting various events. Usually, during the family picnic is when you should have a photo made of the entire family as pictured on this book's cover. It will take a bit of organizing to get everyone positioned correctly. You'll need to secure someone outside the family to take the pictures to include everyone, if the photographer is a family member. Here are some recommendations to get the most out of your group photo shoot. Consider wearing coordinating outfits for the photo, not necessarily matching ones. For instance, everyone could wear khaki pants, shorts, or skirts, and the women could wear light blue polo shirts, while the men wear dark blue ones. Or each family within your large family could wear a different colored shirt (Source: http://www.familylobby.com/family-tips/family-reunion.asp?id=8#tips).

Luminary Ceremony

A luminary ceremony is an event where people gather around with candles or light candles, usually in remembrance of someone who has died. Most family reunions take some time-out to remember deceased loved ones. The procedure for this ceremony includes calling out the name of those who have passed. A representative from that person's family tree branch would light a candle in remembrance of the deceased.

Sing a Composed Family Song

Get in the spirit by making up a family cheer, chant, or song that the whole family can cheer out loud and have fun with. It's a great motivator.

Day Three Reunion Activities

Taking into consideration that most families host a three-day event, the third day of your reunion should not extend past midafternoon to allow out-of-town family members time to catch a plane, train, bus, or drive back home.

Buffet Breakfast or Brunch

A buffet breakfast or brunch can be easily arranged through your host hotel or resort. Generally, breakfast and brunch is less expensive than a dinner meal. To plan this event, you'll need a confirmed head count about two to four weeks prior to the scheduled event. Also, look into the "all you can eat" buffet restaurants chains. More than likely their prices will be less than that charged by hotels or resorts.

Church Service

If you're having your reunion near or around your hometown you might enjoy attending a worship service together at your old home church. Be sure to check out worship times and plan to sit together as a family. You might want to let the church know your family will be there, ahead of time, by calling the office at least three months before your reunion.

Awards and Special Recognition

Create certificates to be passed out to family members. Use your imagination and try to think up as many categories as possible, so that you can recognize the largest amount of family members that you can. Possible recognition categories include these basics. Consider recognizing an elder or younger person of the family and the oldest/newest married couple. Perhaps you can recognize the person who traveled the farthest/shortest distance to the reunion or the family member with the most children. This is a time that you may want to recognize the family members who contributed their time and energy to organize the family reunion. You may choose to verbally recognize people or award them a gift. Certificate and awards can be created from Microsoft Word templates and can look very professional if you have a color printer. You can also purchase them from your local office supply store.

Philanthropy

Do something good while you're gathered as a family. Brainstorm together or designate one or two people to come up with a philanthropic deed for your family to perform. You could collect and donate monies to a deserving high-school student or students who will be attending college or come up with other ideas based on your family's interest.

Family Business Meeting

The family business meeting is held for two main purposes. The first purpose is to decide on the location of the next reunion along with an approximate date. Second, to discuss any other pertinent family business, including future projects such an establishing a scholarship fund, creating a family investment club, making an heirloom quilt, or setting up a family association. It's a good idea to hold reunions consistently each time for planning purposes. For example, if your family decides to have their reunion on the second week of July, then those who work have ample time to request off from work. Remember to rotate locations if you can, to prevent burnout and boredom. It is best to set up regional planning committees in each region where you have enough family meetings (Source: How to Plan a Family Reunion | eHow.com http://www.ehow.com/how_55_family-reunion.html#ixzz1D9WrlCmq).

Reunion Frequency

How often to have subsequent reunions is a decision that should be made by the family at large. The best time to discuss this matter is during the family business meeting. In the same afore-mentioned Reunions Magazine/East Stroudsburg University study, they found that 46 percent of families make the reunion an annual event while 28 percent choose two years between reunions. Those who waited longer periods of times, (over two years) did increase the frequency of their reunions for special events like a milestone anniversary or for an ill family member not likely to make it to the next reunion. Frequency is a serious consideration for the reunion planning committee. One year can pass by quickly while two years allow for some extra breathing room.

Chapter 7

Post-Reunion Activities

Evaluation and Follow-Up

After the reunion, evaluate how it went. Accentuate the positive and celebrate your successes. Iron out the rough spots. Encourage ongoing gatherings and reunions. You'll find that it gets easier to organize and even more fun as time goes on.

You'll want to ask people to give you their honest opinions about the reunion in order to plan an even better one next time, but it's difficult to get a truthful response during a face-to-face discussion. The way to get honest evaluations is to provide a way for them to be anonymous. The easiest way is for you to prepare a short questionnaire in advance, asking questions that don't require a big effort to answer, such as yes/no, but always add a section labeled "remarks or suggestions and leave enough space for them to write the suggestions in. Hand the sheet out before the reunion breaks up. Be sure to indicate you don't want any identifiers—no name, etc., and provide a box for them to deposit the sheet. This way, you'll get a big enough number of answers that you can really find out what most attendees thought. There is a sample post reunion survey in appendix A.

Preserving Reunion Memories

There are a number of ways in which to preserve the memories that were created at your family reunion. Upload photos and videos to your family's Web site, and encourage everyone else to do the same. With free, downloadable software from MyPublisher.com, you can select the best images, add captions, and have an album printed. Send out a survey (while everyone's memories are still fresh) asking people what they liked best about the event, and then you can start planning the next one (Source: http://www.womansday.com/Articles/Family-Lifestyle/How-to-Plan-a-Family-Reunion.html).

Digital Photo Scrapbook

Scrapbooking was mentioned in great detail previously. After your family reunion is over, have the creative person in the family put together a scrapbook of the reunion. Then make copies of the scrapbook to e-mail it everyone.

Family Newsletter

(Source: http://family-reunion.com/)

A family newsletter is a great way to keep in touch with each other between reunions. It doesn't have to be a monthly thing, no, not at all. Two or three times a year is plenty to keep everyone in touch. Today, the traditional paper newsletter is obsolete. Nowadays, newsletters are incorporated into Genealogy software. Topics you might want to write about are the following:

- Birthdays and anniversaries.
- Print new addresses for families that have moved
- Memorial stories on family members who have recently passed away.

Publicize Your Efforts

Consider contacting your local newspaper to do a write-up about your reunion. My brother and I were featured in our local paper back in 1993 after our first national family reunion in Philadelphia, PA. At this time, our local newspaper was featuring local people doing special things and we fit the bill.

Also, Reunions Magazine is always looking to do a write-up about your reunion. Submission guidelines include a brief statement about what's special about your reunion and what will inspire others about your reunion. They request a photo of your family of at least 300 dpi. You can refer to reunionsmag@gmail.com for more information.

Staying in Touch

(Source: http://family-reunion.com/)

In generations long past, many family members lived within only a few miles or even a few blocks of each other. Today, that's not the case. It's not unusual for there to be hundreds of miles between relatives and months between phone calls and letters. Staying united as a family is not easy. Your home computer can make keeping in touch a little bit easier by the following:

- Invite your relatives who have computers to join in a family online chat.

- Send out a family newsletter several times a year.

- Create a family homepage, where you can post family pictures and information.

- Create a family directory, with names, addresses, birthdays, and pictures.

I recommend planning activities between reunions that can also serve as fundraisers such as shopping excursions, bowling/skating parties, bus trips to shows, or sightseeing. If you are looking for an activity that is unique and fun experience, consider hosting a girl's night-in-spa party. This was an activity that I personally enjoyed planning. To keep cost down, everyone can bring a covered dish of finger foods. Any beauty consultant of any company such as Mary Kay, Avon, and Sensaria will be happy to give free demonstrations of the products. Sensaria gives a choice of free foot soaks, hand massage treatment, or facial. The nice thing about being a host is that you can get free products if you guest spends a certain amount; usually $100 or more. I hired a masseuse to provide chair massages. My guests loved this. The going rate for chair massage is about $1 per minutes. For those of you who are not good party planners, there are local spas that host "spa night parties" in your home for a fee depending on the services your guest desires. Prices range from between forty to eighty per person. Typical Spa treatments include hand and feet treatments, hot stone facials, seated chair massage, twenty-five-minute table massage, and body detox treatments. Usually, there is a fifteen guest minimum with 2 treatments per guest.

We can't leave the men out. For the men in your family consider a night out at a sports game, weekend hunting, or fishing. I recommend having activities for children—they love amusement park and cookouts.

Any activity that you plan as a fundraiser can help defray the cost of the expenses for the next reunion. Keep in mind that there are always activities that you can plan to fit everyone's budget. Whether a backyard picnic, family game night, potluck dinner, or cruise to the Caribbean Islands, I have found that it's not what you do at the reunion that has a lasting impact, but what's done after the reunion maintains family unity.

So, in a nutshell, taking your family reunion to the next level doesn't end after you have completed researching your family's history or planned a few successful reunions. In essence, taking your reunion to the next level really is about fostering a sense of connectedness that extends year around, so that your family will be motivated and committed to continue to do whatever it takes to maintain a strong family unit.

Appendix A

Oral History Interview Questionnaire

Name of person interviewed:

Date:

1. What is your family's surname?

2. Do you know the meaning of this surname? Origin?

3. Are there any traditional first names, middle names, or nicknames in your family? Is there a naming tradition?

4. Does your family have any traditions?

5. What stories have come down to you from your parents, grandparents, or other relatives?

6. Have these relatives described their past to you?

7. What have you learned about their childhood, adolescence, schooling, marriage, work, religion, political activity, recreation, etc?

8. How did your parents, grandparents, and or other relatives, come to marry?

9. Are there stories of lost loves, jilted brides, unusual courtships, arranged marriages, elopements, or runaway lovers?

10. Did any historical events affect your family (i.e., wars,

Depression, etc)?

11. What expressions are used in your family?

12. How are holidays celebrated in your family?

13. What holidays are most important—national, religious, or family?

14. Does your family hold reunions? How often? Where? When? Who is invited? Who comes? Who are the organizers?

15. Are there traditional foods, customs, or activities? Are stories exchanged?

16. Are stories or records exchanged?

17. Are record kept? By whom?

18. Have any recipes been preserved in your family from past generations?

19. What was their origin? How were they passed down? Oral? Written?

20. Are they still used today in pure form, or updated.

21. Have other persons been incorporated into your family? Were these people given a title such as aunt or cousin?

22. Is there a family cemetery? Who is buried with whom? Who makes burial place decisions? Are there grave markers? What information is recorded on them?

23. Does anyone in your family save old obituaries or news clippings of obituaries?

24. Does your family have heirlooms or other objects of

sentimental value that have been handed down?

25. Do you know their origin?

26. Does your family have photo albums, scrapbooks, slides, or home movies?

27. Who created them? When are they displayed?

Sample Pre-Reunion Survey

We will be hosting our _____ family reunion in _____ (state). To help the planning committee prepare for this great event, we would like to get your input. Please answer the questions below and mail your response to _____ or call _____ no later than _____ (date).

Name _____

Address _____

City _____ State _____ Zip code _____

Phone number _____ e-mail _____

Are you interested in attending the family reunion? Yes ___ No ___

If yes, how many people will likely attend in your family?

Children ages 0-6 _____

Children ages 7-12 _____

Children ages 13-17 _____

Adults _____

Seniors _____

Seniors over 65 _____

How many days would you like the reunion to be held?

____ Three days ____ Four days ____ Seven days

___ Other

What type of room accommodations will you require?

___ Single (king-size bed)

___ Double (two queen-size beds)

___ Suite

What type of reunion would you be most interested in having?

___ Traditional style (outside city limits/rural setting)

___ Contemporary style (within the city limits/urban setting)

Whether traditional or contemporary style reunion is preferred, what are some of the activities that you would like included in our reunion?

___ Dinner banquet at a hotel   ___ Day trip to local aquarium

___ Picnic in the park   ___ Horse and carriage ride

___ Musical or play   ___ Museum

___ Dinner cruise   ___ Concert

___ Jazz restaurant

___ Amusement park

___ Nightclub outing   ___ Trip to the zoo

___ Casino trip   ___ Sports game

___ Shopping at the mall   ___ City/town tour

___ Other   ___ Other

How would you like to see the family reunion organized? Please indicate which activities you desire or not by placing a yes or no where indicated.

Day 1

___ Registration

___ Welcome reception and get-acquainted night

___ Refreshments

___ Other

Day 2

___ City/town tour

___ Shopping trip

___ Dinner banquet at a hotel

___ Dinner cruise

___ Other

Day 3

___ Breakfast buffet

___ Worship service

___ Dinner

___ Other

What are three of your favorite activities or hobbies you like doing in your free time?

If a Traditional Style reunion is preferred, what are some of the activities would you be most interested?

___ Resort

___ Four day, three-night cruise

If a traditional style reunion is preferred, what activities would you be most interested?

___ Golf

___ Volleyball

___ Hiking

___ Fishing

___ Miniature golf

___ Ping pong

___ Canoeing

___ Ratchet ball

___ Shuffleboard

___ Skating

___ Swimming

___ Horseback riding

___ Soccer

___ Tennis

___ Line dancing

___ Basketball

___ Bicycling

___ Arcade games

___ Badminton

___ Bingo

___ Card games

___ Talent show

___ Fashion show

___ Other

If you would like our reunion to be held at a resort, what type of services/amenities would you like to be offered?

___ Full service spa

___ Live entertainment

___ Health and fitness center

___ Golf package

___ Conference center

___ Internet access

___ Babysitting service

___ All-inclusive meals

___ Souvenir/gift shop

___ Kid's camp

___ Water sports and activities

___ Theater

What is your favorite type of music?

___ R and B   ___ Hip Hop   ___ Opera

___ Contemporary gospel

___ Jazz   ___ Reggae

___ Southern gospel   ___ Blues   ___ Pop

___ Rap   ___ Classical   ___ Hard rock

If you prefer a cruise, which port would you be most interested in visiting?

___ Anguilla   ___ Mexico

___ Antigua and Barbuda   ___ Martinique

___ Barbados   ___ Netherlands Antilles

___ Belize   ___ Jamaica

___ British Virgin Islands   ___ Puerto Rico

___ Cayman Islands   ___ Saint Kitts and Nevis

___ Costa Rica   ___ Saint Lucia

___ Dominica   ___ Trinidad and Tobago

___ Dominican Republic

___ U.S. Virgin Islands

Family Reunion Meeting Agenda

Meeting date/time/location

Attendees/absentees:

Call to order: Meeting opened at ___ a.m. /p.m. by chairperson.

Reading of previous meeting minutes.

A. Meeting minutes accepted as read.

B. Meeting minutes accepted with named corrections.

V. New business

VI. Old business

A. Payment of dues

B. Committee reports

1. Committee/committee head updates

2. Treasurer's report

VII. Next meeting date

Twenty-Four—Month Family Reunion Time Line Planner

Twenty-Four to Eighteen Months Before

- Form reunion planning committee and subcommittees

- Send out pre-reunion survey (reunion planning committee secretary or communication committee)

- Scout out locations and facilities (reunion planning committee or hotel/accomodations committee)

- Start mailing list/family directory (communications committee)

- Develop budget and bookkeeping system (secretary, treasurer, and finance committee)

Twelve Months Before

- Organize mailing system (communications committee)

- Set date for reunion (reunion planning committee)

- Hotel/accomodations Committee chooses reunion location (hotel, resort, or cruise ship)

- Hotel/accomodations committee reserve block of rooms at hotel for attendees

- Activities and food committee hire caterer, photographer, printer, and DJ

- Choose a reunion theme (reunion planning committee)

Nine Months Before

- Schedule events and activities (activities committee)

- Send out first mailing/invitation to include registration form and cost (secretary or communications committee)

Six Months Before

- Start the printing of reunion souvenir booklet (communications committee)
- Confirm reservations, entertainment, and caterers (hotel/accommodations and food committee)
- Send out second invitation mailing (communications committee)

Four to Three Months Before

- Hotel and accommodations committee members meet with hotel staff and visit facility
- Announce event to local news media and elected officials (communications committee)
- Select decorations, signs, banners, and order printed items (food and communications committees)
- Choose menu (food committee)
- Reserve rental equipment (food committee and activities committees)
- Make special assignments such as activities and games so that volunteers have time to prepare and purchase supplies for their assignment (chairperson/president along with activities committee)

Two Months Before

- Reunion chairperson/president oversees detailed schedule

and assignments such as

- Directions on how to get to the reunion site (transportation committee)

- Date, time, and location of the reunion (communications committee)

- Remind family members to bring in their fundraising donations (finance committee)

- Remind family reunion planning subcommittee members of their assignments(chairperson/president)

- Complete the family directory (communications committee)

- Place confirmation call to caterers and photographers (activities, food, and hotel/accomodationscommittees)

- Start purchasing nonperishable items: dry goods, decorations, etc., (activities, food, and hotel/accomodations committees)

One Month Before

- Review final details with family reunion committee/subcommittee (chairperson/president)

- Reconfirm meeting, banquet room accommodations (hotel/accomodations committee)

- Contact restaurants or caterers with a final guest count (hotel/accomodations committee)

- Confirm with relatives who will be bringing food or other Items (chairperson and all committee heads)

One to Two Weeks Before

- Get chairs, tables, grills, and other items (hotel/accomodations and activities committee)
- Buy last-minute decorations (welcome banners and signs) and supplies, perishable items (hotel/accomodations and activities committee)

One Day Before

- Determine facility staff contacts for event (chairperson/president and committee heads)
- Solve last minute problems (chairperson/president and committee heads)
- Review final details with reunion committee (chairperson/president)
- Set up and decorate reunion site (set-up committee)

Day of Reunion

- Post flyers with reunion schedule (set-up committee)
- Set up last minute decorations (set-up committee)
- Welcome family members as they arrive (welcoming committee)

Afterwards

- Reflect and evaluate—note what worked and what didn't
- Complete bookkeeping and settle accounts
- Write thank-you notes to volunteers, hotel staff, caterers, and DJs

(Source: 11th Edition of Reunions Workbook by Reunions Magazine and http:/familyreunionhelper.com/reunion_checklist.php).

Sample Invitation Letter — Nine Months Before Reunion

Date _____

Dear Family:

Well, it's time for us to come together. Many times, when we came together as a family unit, it was not on a joyous occasion. Now is the time for us to meet new offspring, additions to the family, and to become reacquainted again. The family unit is a vital part of our lives, and we need to reemphasize the necessity of a strong family unit. We can make this possible by establishing an annual family reunion. We can build bonds and bridges that were once lost and forgotten. We can make it happen with your help. Your support and input is crucial for making this event successful and memorable.

We, the _____ family reunion committee, have scheduled a tentative date of _____ at _____. This facility is large enough to accommodate us and they have various outdoor activities. We are asking each family member, including yourself, spouse, and children that live with you, without a family of their own, to donate $_____. This cost will cover food, nonalcoholic beverages, and games such as volleyball, softball, jump rope, and other games, especially for children. Also, we would like to have tee shirts made however, the cost of $_____/ shirt will not be included in the $_____ reunion fee. There are so many issues we need to discuss, so please call or e-mail _____, chairperson for the _____ family reunion at (XXX) XXX-

XXXX or e-mail. If he/she is unavailable, just leave a message on his answering machine. If you are interested in attending _____ family reunion, please complete and return the below portion of this letter, with payment to:

Reunion chairperson

Chairperson's mailing address

Name _____

Address _____

City _____ State _____

Number of family members attending:

Adults _____ at $ _____
Children _____ at $ _____

Names of family members attending:

_____

_____
___

_____
___

_____
___

Number of tee-shirts: _____ at $ _____

_____ at $ _____

Adult size: ___ S ___ M ___ L ___ XL ___ XXL ___ XXXL

Children size: ___ S ___ M ___ L

Total payment enclosed: $_____

Will you need hotel accommodations? ___ Yes ___ No

Do you need transportation to the reunion? ___ Yes ___ No

I am unable to attend the reunion. ___ No

Sincerely,

Communications committee

Sample Invitation Letter—Six months Before Reunion

Date _____

Hello Family,   No doubt by now, you've heard about our family reunion. We, the members of the reunion planning committee hope to see each and every one of you during the weekend of _____. We are planning to make this a very memorable occasion beginning with Friday evening straight through Sunday afternoon. So, plan to stay the entire weekend.   The program committee has planned an array of activities that we believe all will enjoy and includes the following:

Day One

Family registration 6:00 p.m.-10:00 p.m.

Welcome reception 6:00 p.m.-9:00 p.m.

Hotel location

Address

City, state

Time

Light hors d'oeuvres served

Day Two

Morning Activities

Continental breakfast 8:00 a.m.-10:30 a.m.

Family picnic 12:00 p.m.-3:00 p.m.

Family group photos

Lot of fun, games, and swimming

Be sure to wear family reunion tee shirts

Family meeting immediately following picnic to make decisions for our next reunion

Evening Activities

Hotel dinner banquet 6:00 p.m.-10:00 p.m.

Presentation of family history

A memorial tribute

Singing of the family song

Sharing of family photo albums

Family group photos

Awards/presentations

Games and give-a-ways

** Dress semiformal**

Day Three—Sunday

Buffet breakfast 8:00 a.m.-10:00 a.m.

Church service 11:00 a.m.-1:00 p.m.

Buffet lunch 1:00 p.m.-3:00 p.m.

If you have any questions or concerns, please contact our reunion chairperson at the following address or phone number:

Chairperson

Chairperson address

Chairperson phone number (s)

With warm affection,

The communications committee

Sample Invitation Letter—Two Months Before Reunion

Date _____

Hello Family,

The hotel and accommodations committee have selected the _____ hotel to host our _____ family reunion. The reservations have been made as follows:

Dates:

Arrival: Friday, _____

Departure: Sunday, August 8, 1993

Guest Rooms:

Single—two-person occupancy $69.00 net rate/room/night

Double—four-person occupancy $69.00 net rate/room/night

All guest rooms are subject to current taxes at the time of arrival. The present tax rate is 14 percent.

Reservations: Individuals will be responsible for their own room charges and reservations. Reservations can be made by calling 1-800-XXX-XXXX. Please inform the hotel staff that you are part of the _____ family group so that you can receive the group rate.

Cutoff Date: All rooms placed in block will be held until three weeks before the first night of arrival. Reservations after the cutoff date will be taken on a space available basis only.

Check-In Time: Friday, _____ at 3:00 p.m.

Checkout Time: Sunday, _____ at 12 noon.

Parking: Parking is included for registered guests of the hotel. Parking is also available to nonregistered guests attending our reunion at an hourly rate.

Location:

_____ Hotel

Address

Phone number

Don't forget, the welcome reception will be held in the _____ Ballroom of the hotel, in the lower lobby from 6:00 p.m. through 9:00 p.m.

Cordially,

The communications committee

Post reunion Survey

E= excellent   G=good   S=satisfactory   US=unsatisfactory

(Please circle your response)

1. How were your hotel accommodations?

E G S US

2. Would you recommend this hotel or resort?

Yes No

3. While visiting _____ (city/town), which activities or places were most interesting to you?

a. Shopping

b. Cultural/historical sites

c. Nightlife/entertainment/water-front activities

4. How would you rate the banquet facilities?

E G S US

5. How would rate your tour guide on the city tour or picnic facilities?

E G S US

6. Would you recommend this tour?

Yes No

7. Was the tour too long?

Yes   No

8. How would you rate the picnic facilities?

   E   G   S   US

9. Were there enough activities offered at the picnic?

Yes   No

10. Would you recommend this picnic facility? Why?

   Yes   No

11. Would you like to have another family reunion in _____ (city/town)?

   Yes   No

12. Please list other activities that you would like to see included in future reunions. What suggestions would you make for future family reunions?

About the author

The author is a nurse practitioner, who initially began researching her family's health history as a personal project to learn more about the conditions and diseases that were prevalent in her family. By knowing the diseases and conditions that were present in her family, Ms. Mason thought that she would be better able to communicate health risks with the goal of helping her family to prevent diseases that may succumb to. Little did she know that over twenty years later, this project would turn into something much more. Not only did she become the family historian, but also functions as one their main genealogical researchers and provides guidance in family reunion planning. Ms. Mason has held membership in the African American Genealogy Group of Philadelphia and has attended The Family Reunion Conferences sponsored by Temple University's Family Reunion Institute, under the direction of Dr. Ione Vargus.

Book Summary

Family Reunion: Taking it to the next level is a step-by-step guide book designed to help both the novice and seasoned family historian and reunion organizer navigate through the process of successful genealogy research and family reunion planning. It was written for those who desire to take their family reunion to the next level; from the backyard to the hotel courtyard, from local to national, and from one branch to multiple branches of the family tree.

Topics Covered

Family history research

How to conduct an oral history interview?

Family trees and genealogy software

Navigating online genealogy databases and records

Genetic genealogy and DNA testing

Preserving and sharing the family history

Developing PowerPoint presentations

Digital photo scrapbooking

Making a family DVD movie

Family reunion planning

Pre-reunion survey

24-Month family reunion timeline planner

Reunion invitations and letters

Organizing reunion planning committees

Responsibilities of the reunion planning committees and subcommittees

Budgeting and financing the reunion

Activities and games

Reunion tee shirts

Reunion souvenir book

Creating a Family Website

www.ingramcontent.com/pod-product-compliance
Lightning Source LLC
Chambersburg PA
CBHW042112120526
44592CB00042B/2703